TUG OF WAR: ME VS THEM

TUG OF WAR: ME VS THEM

A HANDBOOK TO BREAK FREE FROM PLEASING OTHERS AND EMBRACING YOUR TRUE SELF

MARIE HOLLOMAN BRIDGES

Copyright © 2025 by Marie Holloman-Bridges

ISBN: 979-8-9923045-2-7

Library of Congress Control Number

Book Cover Design and Interior Design: Tri Widyatmaka

Back Cover Photography: Cecil Goodwin

Editor: Jessica Gang

Makeup Artist: Trina Petty

Hair by: Salon A'Marie

Printed in the United States of America

1st edition, March 2025

DEDICATION

*T*o those who have felt the weight of the world's expectations, this book is for you.

To the silent warriors battling their own tug-of-war, know you are not alone. This journey is ours, and together, we find resilience.

And finally, those who challenge and push me beyond my limits, thank you for shaping the person I am today. Your presence has been a powerful catalyst for growth and self-discovery.

With gratitude and hope,

Marie Holloman-Bridges

TABLE OF CONTENT

INTRODUCTION

*I*t was Saturday afternoon, and I was in the kitchen preparing for a family gathering. My checklist was impossibly long: appetizers in the oven, decorations half-done, and the guest bathroom waiting for a final touch-up. I was exhausted, but determined to make everything perfect. My family had grand expectations of me—I'd always been the one who made sure everything ran smoothly, and I didn't want to let them down. But on that day, something snapped.

I remember standing over the sink, holding a stack of plates, and feeling my chest tighten. Tears welled up in my eyes as I asked myself, "Why am I doing this? Why am I breaking myself for people who don't notice how much effort I put in?" It wasn't just plates I was holding—it was years of self-neglect. At that moment, the invisible rope of people-pleasing had reached its breaking point.

That day marked the beginning of a journey to untangle the ropes of guilt, fear, and resentment that had kept me bound to others' expectations for so long. It wasn't easy, but it was necessary. Through that journey, I found a life rooted in self-acceptance and inner strength; one where I could finally put myself first without shame or apology. This book is the result of that journey and an invitation for you to begin your own.

Does this sound familiar to you? Have you ever found yourself bending over backward to meet expectations that don't align with your values? Maybe it's an overwhelming desire to keep peace, to avoid conflict, or to gain approval from people who rarely give it. You're not alone. Many of us live in a constant tug-of-war—pulled between the desire to please others and the deep yearning to live authentically. In fact, nearly half of U.S. adults struggle with this tension, with 49 percent identifying as people-pleasers and 92 percent admitting to engaging in at least one people-pleasing behavior (YouGov, 2022).

I know this struggle deeply because it's been my story for as long as I can remember. Growing up, I was the peacemaker, the one who always went along to get along. When my siblings needed something, I gave it up—even when it hurt—because it was easier than enduring their guilt trips or sharp words. Over time, I taught myself to shrink, to prioritize keeping the peace over my own needs. What I didn't realize then was how deeply those patterns would shape my adult life.

As an adult, those same patterns of people-pleasing followed me into relationships, friendships, and even my career. For instance, there was one particularly challenging relationship where I knew I needed to let go but couldn't. Being with this person was both comforting and painful. I gave them everything: my time, my energy, and the best parts of myself, hoping they'd see how much I cared. I convinced myself that if I just gave a little more and held on a little longer, they'd finally recognize my worth. But deep down, I knew this wasn't sustainable. That relationship drained me, leaving me feeling stuck, unfulfilled, and invisible.

It wasn't until I made the courageous decision to let go that I began to reclaim my life and sense of self.

This book, *Tug-of-War: Me vs. Them*, is my story and my guide for you to break free from this endless struggle. It's not a polished roadmap for perfection, but an honest conversation about the messy, beautiful journey toward self-acceptance. Together, we'll uncover the patterns that keep us stuck in cycles of people-pleasing and explore practical ways to reclaim our time, energy, and sense of self.

In the chapters ahead, I'll share how I learned to recognize toxic patterns, set healthy boundaries, and rebuild my self-worth. You'll learn how to step forward lighter, freer, and fully aligned with your true purpose. Picture yourself cutting those ropes—stepping into a life that honors your dreams, values, and worth.

Authoring this book was my act of choosing myself over others' expectations. Now, I'm inviting you to take that same step. Let's begin this journey toward reclaiming yourself and creating the life you deserve together.

PART I:
THE STRUGGLE WITHIN

CHAPTER ONE:

RECOGNIZING THE ROPE

> **"**
>
> *The greatest prison people live in is the fear of what other people think.*—**David Icke**
>
> **"**

I see you. No one else may notice, but I do. Once again, your schedule is packed—not with something you chose, but with something someone else added, and you felt you couldn't say no. This silent struggle is one I know all too well. I call it the invisible rope—the unseen force that keeps pulling us in directions we never intended to go. You feel the pull of this invisible rope, a constant tension guiding your actions and decisions, often against your own desires. This rope isn't tangible, but you feel it pull every day. It tugs at you when you agree to plans you didn't want to make, stay late at work to take on yet another project, or swallow your opinions to avoid conflict. Though no one else sees it, you know it's there—a constant tension pulling you in directions you might not have chosen for yourself.

The rope symbolizes the accumulated weight of others' expectations, societal pressures, and the unspoken rules we've internalized over time. It binds us, often so subtly that we don't even realize how tightly it's wrapped around us until we're stretched to our limits. Like the wind, the rope is invisible, but its effects are undeniable. You may not see the rope, but you feel it in the heaviness of your commitments, the ache of self-neglect, and the exhaustion of living a life dictated by others.

Picture a day when the rope pulls hardest—when you're juggling **deadlines**, tending to family obligations and trying to *keep* up appearances all at once. Each task and expectation adds a new thread, making the rope stronger and harder to untangle. You might think, "If I can just hold on a little longer, everything will fall into place." But instead of easing, the tension grows, leaving you feeling depleted and disconnected from your own needs.

This tug-of-war isn't always dramatic. Sometimes it's a quiet, persistent pull, like the wind whispering through the trees. Other times, it's as relentless as a storm, forcing you to lean in with all your might to avoid being swept away. Yet, regardless of its intensity, the rope is always there, shaping your choices and defining how you show up in the world.

The challenge lies in recognizing the rope as a web of external demands and internalized beliefs that keep you tethered. Only when you recognize the rope, can you begin to loosen its grip and reclaim your autonomy. This chapter will guide you in recognizing where the rope appears in your life, how it has shaped your actions, and how to start untangling its threads.

Isabella's Story: Breaking the Habit of Saying Yes

Isabella was the point of reference in her office. Her coworkers admired her reliability and efficiency, but beneath her calm demeanor was someone grappling with a deep sense of inadequacy and a fear of letting others down. She felt torn between her desire to preserve her reputation and the quiet exhaustion that came from constantly suppressing her own needs to meet the expectations of everyone around her. Isabella's motivation stemmed from a desire to be seen as indispensable, but this came at a cost she hadn't yet realized. Need someone to stay late? Call Isabella. A last-minute project? Isabella would oversee it. Her reputation as dependable and diligent was a badge of honor—and a weight she carried every day.

Her workdays started before sunrise and often ended long after dark. Lunch breaks were a luxury she didn't allow herself. Family dinners became missed moments. She would sit at her desk, her shoulders tight, her stomach knotted, yet she convinced herself it was worth it. This was the prize of success—or so she thought.

One Friday night, Isabella found herself staring at the clock on her computer. It was 9:30 p.m. The office was empty except for her. Papers were scattered across her desk, and the dull hum of fluorescent lights buzzed overhead. She had just finished reworking a presentation—one she had agreed to redo because her boss casually mentioned it could be "a bit better."

Exhaustion overwhelmed her as she leaned back in her chair, her eyes stinging from hours on the screen. She reached for her phone to text her husband that she'd be late again when a sharp thought interrupted: *Why am I doing this? Why does everyone else's opinion matter more than my well-being?* For the first time, she felt a small spark of determination to make a change. That single moment became a turning point. She felt a quiet pride in prioritizing herself and discovered strength she didn't know she had.

The next morning, Isabella made a choice. When her boss approached her with yet another last-minute assignment, she took a deep breath and said, "I'd love to help, but my current workload won't allow me to give this project the attention it deserves. Perhaps someone else can assist."

To her surprise, her boss acknowledged, thanked her for her honesty, and found another solution. Isabella felt a quiet sense of relief and pride. This was the first time she prioritized herself at work without feeling like she had to apologize.

Over the following weeks, she began setting boundaries. She politely declined tasks that didn't align with her priorities and started leaving the office on time. She even carved out a lunch break to walk outside and breathe. At first, saying no felt uncomfortable—guilt nagged at her—but each small step toward balance made her stronger.

Isabella realized that her value wasn't tied to how much she sacrificed. By prioritizing herself, she didn't just reclaim her time and energy, she also found a renewed sense of confidence and joy in her work.

My Own Invisible Rope: A Personal Anecdote

For years, I wore reliability like a badge of honor, tightly woven into the invisible rope of expectations that kept me tethered to the approval of others. I was the person everyone could count on—the dependable colleague, the peacemaker in my family, the friend who always said yes. But deep down, I wasn't driven solely by generosity or a sense of duty. The truth was harder to face. I was afraid of what would happen if I didn't meet those expectations.

One moment stands out vividly. It was a Monday evening, and I had just returned home after an exhausting day at work. My phone buzzed with a text from a friend: "Hey, I need a huge favor. Can you help me with something tonight?" I hesitated. I was worn out, mentally and physically, but my instinct kicked in—the automatic, unthinking "yes" that had become my default response.

I spent the next three hours helping my friend, completely sidelining my own needs. When I finally collapsed into bed that night, a wave of frustration washed over me. I wasn't angry at my friend—I was angry at myself. Why did I say yes when every fiber of my being screamed no?

The answer lay in the invisible rope I had been carrying for years, a rope woven from the need to avoid disappointment, to preserve harmony, to be seen as dependable at all costs. Realizing this was like stepping into a spotlight that illuminated years of quiet compromises. At first, I felt an overwhelming sense of vulnerability, as though letting go of the rope would leave me exposed. But soon, I began to see this awareness as a doorway to freedom—a chance to reshape how I valued myself beyond others' expectations. I realized I had tied my worth to the approval of others, and every time I pulled the rope tighter, I was losing a little more of myself.

The turning point came a few months later when I found myself in a comparable situation at work. My boss approached me with a new project—one that was outside my responsibilities and far beyond my bandwidth. My first instinct was to accept, to prove my commitment. But this time, I paused and asked myself, "What's the cost?"

I took a deep breath and said, "I appreciate the opportunity, but I'm at capacity right now. If we can delegate this to someone else or revisit it later, I'll be able to maintain the quality we aim for." To my relief, my boss agreed and assured me it wasn't an issue.

In that moment, I felt the rope begin to loosen. It wasn't a grand declaration or a dramatic change, but it was a small, powerful step toward reclaiming my time and energy. Letting go of the need to please didn't come easily, and I still catch myself reaching for that rope. But with each boundary I set, I remind myself that saying no to others can mean saying yes to myself—and that's a trade worth making.

The Impact of the Rope

The rope isn't confined to our professional lives; it winds its way into relationships, families, and friendships. For example, in a family setting, it might look like taking on every holiday responsibility to ensure everything is perfect or constantly mediating disputes to keep peace. These actions often lead to feelings of exhaustion and resentment as the effort to keep harmony comes at the expense of your own well-being. These moments can add threads to the rope, tying you further into patterns of self-neglect. I remember being in a particularly challenging relationship where I gave everything—my time, energy, and the best parts of myself—hoping they'd see how much I cared. Each time I considered leaving, the thought of losing that attachment pulled me back. I convinced myself that if I just gave a little more, they'd finally recognize my worth.

Looking back, I see now that my attempts to please were like pouring water into a bottomless well—it was never enough. Instead of fulfillment, I found exhaustion, frustration, and a growing sense of invisibility. Staying in that dynamic wasn't just draining—it was holding me back from the life I deserved. Letting go of that rope was one of the hardest and most freeing decisions I've ever made. Vulnerable and uncertain, I stepped into the unknown, only to find clarity and the strength to prioritize myself.

Starting to Untangle Your Rope

Think about your invisible rope. Where do you feel it pull the most? Is it at work, in your relationships, or with your family? Reflect on the last time you said yes to something that didn't feel right. What emotions surfaced—guilt, fear, or pressure to please? Pause and reflect. Recognizing these patterns is the first step to loosening the rope's grip.

In her book, *The Dance of Connection*, Psychologist Harriet Lerner reminds us that living true to ourselves is a deliberate practice of aligning with our values.

Recognizing these moments often starts with noticing when your actions feel misaligned with your inner voice or when you feel a persistent sense of unease about a decision. When we honor our needs and voice our truths, even in uncomfortable moments, we take a step closer to authentic living. For instance, imagine a moment when you're asked to take on yet another commitment, and instead of saying yes out of obligation, you take a deep breath and reply, "I'd love to help, but I need to honor my current priorities right now." As Lerner explains, setting boundaries doesn't have to be a confrontation—it's a quiet affirmation of your values and self-worth, creating space for genuine connection.

Claiming Your Power

As you begin unbraiding the threads of this rope— saying no when it matters, honoring your needs, and reclaiming your energy—you'll feel its weight lift. Each thread released brings you closer to a life of freedom, joy, and self-respect. Let's start this journey together, one intentional step at a time.

Right now, you might be wondering, *"Can I really do this? I've tried setting boundaries before, but it never seemed to stick."* Or perhaps a quiet voice in your mind is whispering doubts: *"What if I let someone down? What if it makes things worse?"* These thoughts are natural—the rope has been part of your life for so long that imagining freedom from it can feel overwhelming or even impossible. But what if the secret lies not just in what you do, but in understanding why the rope is there in the first place? What if loosening its grip starts with uncovering the beliefs, fears, and patterns that have quietly woven it together?

When you begin to see how these threads were formed—how expectations, both external and internal, have shaped your choices—you'll unlock the clarity needed to untangle them. This process isn't about making quick fixes but about creating meaningful change that aligns with your deepest values and restores your sense of self. Awareness is the first step, and with it comes the power to reclaim your life on your terms.

As we move forward, we'll take that first step together by deepening our understanding of how the invisible rope came to be.

CHAPTER **TWO**:

THE ROOTS OF THE ROPE

Understanding and Uncovering Past Influences

> *You have to decide what your highest priorities are and have the courage— pleasantly, smilingly, nonapologetically, to say 'no' to other things.*—**Stephen Covey**

*L*ife shapes us long before we're aware of it. Family expectations, cultural values, and subtle moments of praise often plant seeds that grow into lifelong behaviors. Many of these patterns—like the tendency to please others—take root in childhood and become second nature. Over time, they form what I call "The Rope," a web of influences that bind us to others' expectations, leaving us disconnected from our own desires.

Think of a tree with deep, sprawling roots, anchoring it firmly to the ground. Imagine a young child planting a seed in the backyard, carefully watering it every day because they're told it will grow into something beautiful. Over time, that tree grows, just as the habits and beliefs instilled in us take hold and shape who we become. These roots started as small, fragile threads but grew stronger over time, pulling nutrients from the soil and shaping the tree's growth. Similarly, our early experiences influence our thoughts, behaviors, and decisions, even before we're fully aware of their impact. To untangle the rope, we must trace it back to where it all began—to the moments when approval, praise, and external validation first took root in our lives.

The Roots of My Rope

As a child, I lived for the smile my grandmother gave me when I completed small chores. Her words—"Good girl"—made me feel seen, valued, and loved. Every time she praised my helpfulness, it was like a warm glow lighting up my little world.

I carried that need for validation into every area of my life. At school, I became a model student, always polite, following every rule, working tirelessly to please my teachers. Later, in the military, I took on extra tasks, determined to be seen as dependable and capable. It wasn't until much later that I realized these habits weren't just about being responsible, they were about proving my worth to others.

Even in my marriage, I would announce every small task I completed, hoping for acknowledgment. My husband would laugh and say, "You don't have to tell me every little thing—I can see it!" Once, he teased, "Guess what? I just swept the steps!" It was a lighthearted moment, but it became a meaningful touchpoint. Why did I feel the need to declare my efforts so loudly? The answer lay in those early years, where love and approval felt conditional, something to be earned through good behavior and self-sacrifice.

Brené Brown, in her book *The Gifts of Imperfection*, likens this to carrying a twenty-ton shield—crafted to protect us from judgment but weighing us down in the process. She explains that perfectionism, much like people-pleasing, often originates from a desire to earn approval and acceptance. Gabor Maté expands on this connection in *When the Body Says No*, showing how emotional stress from self-sacrifice manifests as physical ailments like chronic pain and fatigue. For instance, the constant tension in my shoulders wasn't just a physical ailment—it was my body's way of signaling the emotional weight I had been carrying for years. When I began to let go of the need for perfection, I noticed small but profound changes. My headaches became less frequent, and I felt a lightness I hadn't experienced in years. Letting go wasn't easy, but each step brought me closer to a more balanced and fulfilling life.

For years, I ignored my body's signals—the exhaustion, the tension in my shoulders, the pounding headaches that seemed to come out of nowhere. These weren't just random ailments; they were my body's way of saying, "Enough." Recognizing this pattern isn't about assigning blame to our families or past experiences—it's about making conscious choices moving forward. Letting go of these habits isn't just about emotional freedom, it's a step toward reclaiming physical well-being and vitality.

Society's Influence

While childhood experiences plant the seeds of people-pleasing, societal norms nurture their growth. Many of us grew up in cultures or communities that celebrate compliance, respectability, and self-sacrifice, where putting others first is considered a virtue. This leaves little room to prioritize our needs without feeling selfish or guilty.

Take, for example, the comedian who uses humor to win approval in a household where their voice often goes unheard. Or the impeccably dressed individual who seeks validation through appearances, equating external praise with self-worth. Social media amplifies this pressure, presenting curated versions of success and selflessness that can leave us feeling inadequate or disconnected from our authentic selves. For instance, consider the parents scrolling through images of perfectly decorated birthday parties and spotless homes, feeling pressured to meet an impossible standard. These curated moments send the subtle message that anything less than perfection is not enough, fueling a cycle of comparison and self-doubt.

This pressure is compounded by societal expectations around gender, culture, and socioeconomic status. In some cultures, prioritizing others is seen as essential for maintaining harmony, while in others, self-sacrifice may carry a deeply ingrained sense of honor. Gender also plays a significant role; women often face expectations to be caregivers, while men may feel pressured to prove their worth through financial success. Socioeconomic conditions can intensify these behaviors, particularly when financial or social survival depends on meeting others' expectations.

Generational values also play a role. Baby Boomers, raised in an era of economic growth and traditional family structures, often prioritize hard work and duty. For many, skipping vacations or putting self-care on the back burner isn't just a habit—it's a reflection of their dedication. Taking a break can feel indulgent, even irresponsible. You may have seen it in your own family— parents or grandparents who worked tirelessly, rarely taking time for themselves, wearing their sacrifices as a badge of honor. The belief that perseverance and sacrifice define success has been deeply ingrained, making it difficult to prioritize personal well-being without guilt.

Millennials and Gen Z, shaped by technology, economic uncertainty, and evolving social norms, may face different pressures, including the expectation to "perform" on social media or balance personal authenticity with professional success. Celebrities and influencers frequently share their struggles with burnout, feeling the need to maintain a perfect image online while privately battling stress and exhaustion. Think about the influencer who always looks effortlessly put together, constantly traveling and posting curated content—but behind the scenes, they're overwhelmed, exhausted, and desperately trying to keep up. Or the young professional who stays late at work, not because they want to, but because hustle culture tells them they should. The pressure to keep up—whether with career milestones, social trends, or an ever-curated digital presence—creates a modern version of the same cycle of overcommitment and self-neglect, just in a different form.

How might your cultural background, gender, or social standing have influenced your own tendencies? For those navigating intersecting identities—race, gender, sexuality, or ability—these influences may compound, shaping unique patterns of behavior. Reflecting on these nuances can reveal layers of the rope you may not have considered before.

Recognizing Your Patterns

People-pleasing doesn't look the same for everyone. It takes on different shapes based on our experiences, relationships, and emotional needs. You may recognize yourself in one of these profiles—or perhaps see elements of each in your behavior.

- **Amelia – The High Achiever:** Amelia grew up in a household where success was celebrated, and failure was quietly swept under the rug. As an adult, she constantly overcomes herself at work, striving to be the best and fearing she'll lose respect if she doesn't deliver. Her relentless pursuit of validation leaves little time for her own well-being.

- **Justin – The Mediator:** In Justin's family, conflict was a constant presence. As a child, he became the peacemaker, smoothing over disagreements and ensuring everyone got along. Now, as an adult, Justin avoids confrontation at all costs, even if it means sacrificing his own happiness.

- **Naomi – The Caretaker:** Naomi grew up caring for her mother, who had a chronic illness. Her selflessness became a source of pride and identity, but it also taught her to put others' needs before her own. As an adult, Naomi struggles to make space for herself in her relationships, often feeling drained and unappreciated.

These profiles illustrate the many ways the rope manifests in our lives. Take a moment to reflect: Which of these profiles resonates most with you? Can you identify moments when you've acted like Amelia, Justin, or Naomi? Understanding these patterns can help you take the first steps toward change.

Reflection: Recognizing the Roots

Think about the threads of your own story. Whose approval have you been chasing, and why? Perhaps it's a parent, a mentor, or even societal ideals that have shaped your decisions. How have cultural or community values influenced your sense of obligation? Do you notice a difference in how these expectations affect you based on your gender, socioeconomic background, or personal identity? How do generational values—like those of Baby Boomers, Millennials, or Gen Z—shape the way you perceive and respond to these expectations?

Reflect on the stories you've told yourself about your worth—stories that may be rooted deeply in your beliefs and behaviors. What small step can you take today to start loosening this rope?

Setting the Stage for Change

Recognizing the origins of your people-pleasing tendencies lays the groundwork for meaningful transformation. It's not about assigning blame; it's about awareness. By examining how family influences, societal expectations, and individual experiences have shaped your invisible rope, you gain the clarity to question what no longer serves you. Self-awareness empowers you to prune away these threads and create space for growth.

As you pause to reflect on these patterns, you might wonder, *Can I really untangle this? What if it's too late?*

But it's never too late to begin. With each small step—each boundary set, each truth honored—you move closer to reclaiming your life on your own terms. This journey is about discovering what freedom, balance, and authenticity mean for you, and having the courage to live by those values.

CHAPTER **THREE**:

THE OPPONENTS — ME VERSUS THEM

> 66
>
> *Owning our story and loving ourselves through that process is the bravest thing that we'll ever do—**Brené Brown***
>
> 99

*I*t was Thanksgiving, and as usual, I found myself at the center of chaos. My home has an open-concept design, so the dining area, kitchen, and living room blend into one active space. For over twenty years, I've been the one naturally expected to take the lead— ensuring the food was consistently supplied in the chafing dishes, beverages were replenished, plenty of delicious dessert was available, and both children and family friends were accommodated. On top of that, I was typically managing incoming phone calls, text messages, and directions, as I host over eighty people each year.

That day, as I moved from one task to another—cooking, cleaning, and extinguishing metaphorical fires—I felt the weight of it all. Requests kept coming: someone needed a drink refilled, another asked when the turkey would be done, and tensions began to rise as the family dynamics played out. Every demand felt like another thread in the rope, binding me tighter to the expectations of others. With each new task, I felt a growing sense of frustration and weariness, as if the walls were closing in and my own needs were shrinking into the background. It was no longer just me helping; it became *me against them*—their needs pulling so strongly that my own had no room to exist.

At some point, it became too much. I was overwhelmed, scrubbing dishes while others enjoyed the meal I'd prepared. Even guests who weren't family could see my stress. A few approached me, confused by the sight of me cleaning alone, and asked why I hadn't asked for help. Their question struck a nerve, making me realize how much I had taken on without asking for help.

Why hadn't I asked? Was it because I believed it was my responsibility—or because I had taught others to expect it of me? Reflecting later, I realized the answer was a mix of both. I had internalized the idea that my value came from being everything to everyone, and I had unconsciously reinforced that expectation in others. The thought that someone might view me as incapable or unhelpful held me back.

In that moment of quiet bravery, I decided to let go of the need to manage it all. I began delegating tasks to those who offered, trusting them to oversee the cleanup and other responsibilities. And do you know what? The world didn't fall apart. The turkey got carved, the dishes were cleaned, and I even found a moment to sit down and enjoy being present with my family.

This wasn't about rejecting my loved ones or shirking responsibility. It was about recognizing my limits and choosing to honor them. Bravery isn't always a grand, defiant act. Sometimes, it's found in small, deliberate decisions—like allowing myself to let go of the need to do it all and trusting others to share the load. That Thanksgiving moment was a turning point, showing me how the constant pull of others' expectations can overshadow our own needs. That realization during Thanksgiving mirrored a larger truth in my life: the constant tug-of-war between others' expectations and my own needs. In the days that followed, I began to reflect on how often I allowed these expectations to dictate my actions. Slowly, I started making small but meaningful changes—pausing before agreeing to every request, prioritizing tasks that aligned with my values, and giving myself permission to step back when I felt overwhelmed. This tug-of-war is not just about tasks—it's about identity.

The Two Ends of the Rope

Imagine yourself holding onto a thick, rough rope stretched tightly between two ends. On one end, you stand with your values, desires, and boundaries firmly in hand. On the other end, the demands of family, friends, colleagues, and society pull persistently, sometimes overpoweringly, in the opposite direction.

This tug-of-war isn't about physical strength. It's a struggle of identity. Each pull challenges your sense of self-worth, boundaries, and bravery. The question becomes: How do you honor yourself without letting go of meaningful connections?

Understanding the Forces at Play

This tug-of-war often brings us to a crossroads between two fundamental needs: the desire to live authentically and the fear of disappointing others.

Society has conditioned many of us to equate our worth with how much we give, how agreeable we are, or how well we meet expectations. From an early age, many of us are taught to equate busyness with success and compliance with virtue, creating a lifelong pattern of putting others' needs before our own. But this conditioning comes at a cost: emotional exhaustion and an eroded sense of self-worth. Every time we surrender our end of the rope, there's a cost. Over time, this pattern leads to burnout, resentment, and a profound disconnection from us.

In *The 7 Habits of Highly Effective People*, Stephen Covey introduces the concept of the Circle of Influence, teaching us to focus on what lies within our control. Similarly, the tug-of-war between Me vs. Them invites us to examine where our time and energy are being pulled—and to protect our priorities in a way that aligns with our values.

This constant pull of societal expectations and internalized beliefs doesn't just challenge our identity, it takes a toll on our emotional and physical well-being, as we'll explore next.

Consider the story of Nora, a committed professional who poured countless hours into her job, determined to prove her value by always going above and beyond. She worked late nights, took on extra responsibilities, and never said no—all in hopes of receiving recognition. One evening, as Nora sat alone in her office, she realized that no amount of extra work seemed to change how she felt. The exhaustion in her body mirrored the emptiness she felt inside. The next day, she left the office at 5 p.m. for the first time in years—a small but bold step toward reclaiming her peace.

Nora's story is a reminder that people-pleasing often comes at a high price—one that compounds over time, leaving us drained and disconnected. What about you? Have you ever found yourself trading your inner peace for the sake of feeling validated? Reflect on how these moments have shaped your sense of self and consider the steps you can take to reclaim your energy and priorities. This constant surrender doesn't just wear you down physically—it chips away at your confidence, leaving you feeling unseen, unheard, and unworthy of prioritizing yourself.

Self-Worth and Boundaries: The Strength to Hold Your Ground

One of the most vital tools in standing firm is knowing your self-worth and setting healthy boundaries. People-pleasers often struggle with boundaries because they equate maintaining harmony with avoiding conflict.

But self-worth isn't determined by how much we do for others. It's rooted in respect for who we are. When we value ourselves, we communicate that our needs are as important as anyone else's.

Respect begins within. When you respect yourself, others begin to see you as more than just what you provide. In a world that often rewards overcommitment, standing firm in your boundaries can feel countercultural—but it's essential for cultivating self-worth. In my own life, I noticed that as I prioritized my needs and communicated my boundaries, my relationships became more balanced and fulfilling. People began to value my presence and input, not just my ability to manage tasks. Your value becomes rooted in who you are, not just what you can do.

For instance, setting a boundary might look like declining to host a large family event when your schedule is already packed. This decision can be liberating and affirm your right to prioritize yourself.

Letting Go of Guilt

Letting go of guilt isn't easy. It's a practice—a deliberate decision to rewrite the narratives we've been conditioned to follow.

Guilt often whispers that saying no makes us selfish, that we've let someone down. But guilt is also a signal: it shows us where our boundaries are being challenged. Instead of viewing it as something to fear, see it as a signpost pointing toward growth. Nora's story illustrates how guilt can keep us trapped in a cycle of overcommitment. She believed saying no might harm her reputation or relationships, but by taking that bold step to leave the office on time, she began rewriting her internal narrative.

Some people are more prone to guilt due to upbringing, personality, or a powerful desire to maintain harmony. Others, perhaps those with higher self-assuredness or different social conditioning, may feel guilt less acutely. Understanding these dynamics can help you better navigate your own feelings.

To overcome guilt:

1. **Acknowledge it** – Understand where it comes from. Is it tied to unrealistic expectations?

2. **Reframe it** – Replace thoughts like "I'm letting them down" with "I'm honoring myself."

3. **Take small steps** – Start by saying no in low-stakes situations to build confidence.

Each time you respect your boundaries, you strengthen your self-worth. Guilt may linger, but with practice, its hold weakens.

Reflection:
Who's on The Other End of Your Rope?

Take a moment to reflect on who or what is at the other end of your rope. Why do their expectations hold so much weight in your life? Reflect on how these influences have shaped your decisions and what small steps you can take to realign with your values.

Example Exercise:

1. **Identify the Influences** – Write down three people or situations that frequently "pull your rope."

2. **Analyze the Impact** – For each, answer:
   - "What do they expect of me?"
   - "How do I feel when I try to meet these expectations?"
   - "What assumptions am I making about their needs versus my own?"

3. **Set a Boundary** – Write one small action you can take to honor your values and limit the pull of this influence.

Letting go isn't about rejection; it's about clarity. Each time you honor your needs, you create space for balance and fulfillment.

Closing Thoughts

The tug-of-war between Me vs. Them reveals the challenge of balancing others' expectations with your own needs. Letting go isn't giving up—it's about gaining clarity and reclaiming your sense of self. Every small act of courage, whether it's saying no, valuing yourself, or setting a boundary, strengthens your ability to live authentically. True strength lies in letting go of what no longer serves you and embracing what truly matters. For example, saying no to an overbearing obligation might open the space to pursue a passion project or spend quality time with loved ones. Start small—one deliberate step at a time—and watch how these choices ripple into every corner of your life.

Next, we'll explore "Strategies for Letting Go of The Rope," offering practical steps to ease the pressure and create the life you deserve.

PART II:
RECLAIMING YOUR POWER

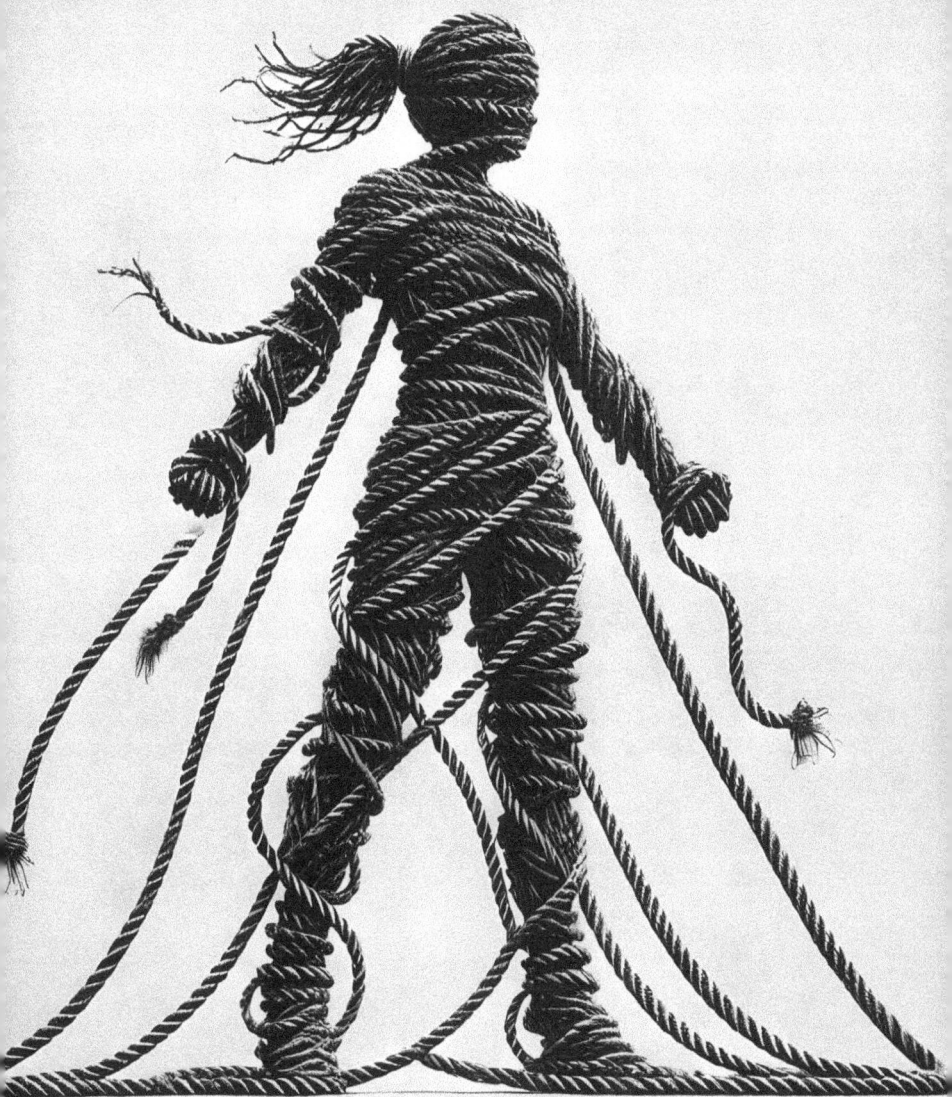

CHAPTER FOUR:

STRATEGIES FOR LETTING GO OF THE ROPE

> *Sometimes letting go is an act of far greater power than defending or holding on.—**Eckhart Tolle***

"Winners never quit, and quitters never win." You've probably heard this phrase repeatedly—a mantra meant to inspire perseverance and dedication. But what if that statement isn't entirely true?

Winners quit all the time. The difference is, they quit the things that no longer serve them. They let go of what drains them, misaligns with their values, or prevents them from stepping into something better. And as a result, they win more.

But quitting often comes with judgment. Walking away from a job, a relationship, or an expectation placed upon you can make it look like you've failed. Others may see it as weakness, a lack of endurance, or an inability to "stick it out." The truth, however, is the opposite. Letting go is not about failing, it's about choosing yourself. It's about recognizing that true strength is found in knowing when to release what no longer aligns with your well-being.

Imagine walking through a dense forest, holding a rope tied to a boulder that slows your every step. The rope burns against your palms as you drag the heavy weight behind you. Each step forward feels harder than the last. You convince yourself that letting go would mean failure, abandonment, or weakness. But what if true strength lies not in enduring the weight but in the courage to release it?

Letting go is not about giving up; it's about choosing freedom over struggle. It's recognizing that clinging to what drains you doesn't make you strong—it holds you back. Releasing weight doesn't mean you've failed; it means you've made room for growth and renewal.

The Moment I Let Go

I remember the end of a relationship that I had poured my heart and soul into. We had been together for years, and I kept hoping things would get better if I could just be more patient, more understanding, or somehow "fix" the growing distance between us. I was constantly on edge, replaying conversations in my mind, wondering what I could have done differently or how I could have bridged the gap between us.

I felt the weight of holding onto something that wasn't giving me peace, yet the thought of letting go filled me with dread. After all, wasn't love supposed to mean staying through the hard times? If I let go, wasn't I admitting failure?

This fear wasn't just about the relationship, it was about the narrative I had internalized. Society often tells us that "winners never quit," and that perseverance is the hallmark of strength. Letting go felt like breaking the rules, as though I was giving up on something I should have fought harder to save.

One night, after yet another exhausting argument, I found myself sitting alone, drained and defeated. The realization came to me in a quiet whisper: I was clinging to a version of the relationship that no longer existed. By holding on, I wasn't just losing my partner, I was losing myself.

That night, I made the choice to release the grip I had on something that no longer aligned with who I was. I allowed myself to step back, to let go of the need to control the outcome, to stop trying to force something that had already run its course. It wasn't a moment of defeat; it was a moment of profound freedom. I felt a sense of relief washing over me, as though a heavy weight had lifted.

Letting go wasn't about giving up—it was about reclaiming myself. It was a decision to prioritize my peace, my worth, and my ability to move forward. That one decision was the first domino in a series of changes that brought clarity and a renewed sense of purpose.

Releasing the Rope: Freedom in Action

Releasing what drains you isn't just about walking away, it's about stepping into a world of freedom and possibilities waiting on the other side.

Consider the story of Grace, a marketing executive who felt trapped in a high-pressure job. While her journey echo's themes of change and release, her unique struggle lies in how she redefined success on her own terms—a critical distinction that sets her apart. Just as my journey showed me the value of reclaiming myself, Grace's story highlights how redefining success can lead to personal and professional fulfillment. Every day, she clung to the belief that quitting would mean failure. But the job drained her, leaving no room for creativity or joy. When Grace finally made the decision to leave, she discovered a new sense of possibility. Her energy returned, her relationships improved, and she started a business that aligned with her values. Choosing to step away allowed her to reclaim her sense of purpose and find fulfillment.

Tara Brach, in her book *Radical Acceptance*, beautifully captures the essence of release. She describes the act of letting go as "touching the ground of being," where we embrace what is and allow ourselves to rest in awareness, free from the grasp of judgment and resistance. This shift doesn't mean we stop caring, it means we stop clinging.

Grace's journey shows us that releasing what no longer serves us isn't just about leaving something behind, it's about stepping into something better. When we unburden ourselves from what depletes us, we make room for what nourishes us.

Subtle Benefits of Release

As you create distance from what once weighed you down, subtle but powerful changes begin to appear in your life. These shifts may not happen all at once, but they accumulate, transforming your emotional and mental landscape. These benefits are just the beginning; they create the foundation for resilience, the key to embracing life's challenges with clarity and strength.

For Grace, leaving her job not only opened doors to a more fulfilling career but also brought unexpected benefits: she became more present with her family and found a renewed sense of creativity. Similarly, I, after releasing that relationship, rediscovered a clarity and self-worth I hadn't realized I'd lost.

This shift isn't limited to work or relationships. I recall a time when I clung to a rigid fitness routine, driven by the belief that more effort equaled better results. I ignored signs of burnout and injury, convincing myself that stopping or changing my approach would mean failure. When I finally embraced a more balanced mindset, I found that I enjoyed my workouts more and saw better results.

The benefits of release are woven into our experiences:

- A calmer mind as the anxiety of holding on dissipates.
- Deeper connections with others, built on mutual respect rather than control.
- Renewed creativity and focus, as mental space is freed from unresolved burdens.
- A profound sense of peace, knowing you've prioritized your well-being.

These aren't just hypothetical outcomes—they are the quiet revolutions that happen when we choose ourselves over the weight we've been carrying.

Lightening the Load

Paris, a mother of two, often felt like she was drowning in the never-ending demands of her life—work deadlines, family responsibilities, and social expectations. Unlike Grace, Paris's journey centered on subtle mental shifts rather than major life changes.

One evening, after her children had gone to bed, she closed her eyes and imagined herself in a boat on a calm lake. She felt the cool breeze on her face and heard the soft lapping of water against the boat. In her mind, she saw herself tossing overboard the unnecessary baggage she'd been carrying: the pressure to be perfect, the fear of disappointing others, and the guilt over setting boundaries. She imagined the splash of each item hitting the water and the ripples spreading outward, symbolizing the freedom and possibility she was creating with every release. Paris felt her chest loosen and her breath deepen.

Inspired by this small mental shift, she began making real changes. She started delegating tasks, setting boundaries with her time, and letting go of the need to say yes to everything. Over time, Paris realized that releasing these burdens didn't mean she cared less, it meant she could care more about the things that truly mattered.

Paris's story reminds us that letting go isn't an act of abandonment, it's an act of empowerment. It's about choosing where to place your energy and creating a space for peace and purpose.

The Value of Resilience

Letting go isn't just about removing burdens—it's about creating space for something greater. Unlike the tug-of-war in Chapter 3, which focused on the internal struggle of holding on, this chapter explores release as a pathway to transformation. When you free yourself from what no longer aligns with your well-being, you make room for resilience to take root and flourish.

Resilience is your ability to adapt, recover, and grow in the face of life's challenges. It's not just about bouncing back, it's about moving forward with clarity and purpose. Often, we don't realize the depth of our resilience until we step away from what weighs us down. It isn't about enduring hardship for the sake of endurance; it's about recognizing when to pivot, when to adjust, and when to embrace new possibilities. Each time you release what holds you back, you reinforce your ability to navigate life on your terms.

Ways to Release:

1. **Write a Letter or Message**:
   Sometimes, articulating your feelings in writing helps clarify your intentions and sets the stage for release. Whether you send it or not, the act of writing can be therapeutic.

   Refined Sample Email/Text:
   Hi [Name], I've been reflecting on some recent changes in my priorities and well-being. I realize I need to focus more on aligning with what feels right for me. I deeply value the times we've shared, but I think it's time for me to step back. Thank you for understanding, and I wish you all the best moving forward.

2. **Declutter Your Space:**

   Releasing physical clutter often mirrors emotional release. Letting go of items tied to past chapters in your life can be a powerful symbolic act.

3. **Set Boundaries:**

   Start small by saying no to a minor obligation or request. Each boundary you set reinforces your self-worth and creates space for what truly matters.

4. **Try Visualization:**

   Like Paris, close your eyes and imagine yourself releasing your burdens one by one. Picture them drifting away, leaving you lighter and freer.

5. **Seek Support:**

   Share your journey with a trusted friend, therapist, or mentor. Talking about your decision to release can provide clarity and encouragement.

Creating Space for Resilience

Releasing what no longer serves you is more than an act of letting go—it's an act of renewal. It allows resilience to emerge in new and unexpected ways, helping you stand firm when life challenges your newfound freedom.

For instance, after Grace walked away from her high-pressure job, she faced uncertainty, but over time, her resilience strengthened. With each challenge, she gained confidence, built a business aligned with her values, and reclaimed her sense of purpose. Choosing to step away didn't weaken her—it allowed her to become more of who she was meant to be.

By freeing yourself from what drains you, you don't just create space—you create opportunity. Resilience will be your anchor as you move forward, helping you build a life that truly reflects your values and aspirations.

As you step into this next phase, reflect on these questions:

- What can I do with the space I've created?

- How will I use this freedom to align more closely with my values?

- Who do I want to become now that the weight is lifted?

- What is one small, specific action I can take today to release something that no longer serves me?

These questions aren't meant to pressure you; they're an invitation to envision the possibilities that lie ahead. Making space for growth isn't a loss, it's an act of self-trust. It's not about quitting; it's about choosing yourself. Winners quit all the time. They walk away from what no longer serves them to make room for what truly matters. By stepping away from what depletes us, we're not giving up, we're giving ourselves the gift of freedom.

Releasing burdens is just the first step. True transformation requires not only the courage to move on but also the strength to stay aligned with your truth. As we move forward, we'll explore the inner resilience needed to maintain this freedom. Walking away from what holds you back is powerful, but standing firm in your decision is where lasting change begins. Together, we'll uncover the tools to stand firm and remain steadfast, even when life's challenges pull you back into the tug-of-war.

CHAPTER FIVE:

BUILDING STRENGTH TO HOLD YOUR GROUND

> " *To be yourself in a world that is constantly trying to make you something else is the greatest accomplishment.—* **Ralph Waldo Emerson** "

*I*nner strength is like the unshakable roots of a tree. No matter how fiercely the wind blows or how heavy the rain falls, the tree stays standing because its roots run deep. Similarly, cultivating resilience allows us to stay grounded through life's storms. Consider Rosa Parks, who stood firm in her values during a time of immense societal pressure. Her inner strength became a symbol of resilience, inspiring generations to hold their ground in the face of adversity.

Rather than just committing to resilience, the true test lies in consistency—staying aligned with your values and priorities even when temptations to revert arise. Consistency is what transforms inner strength into a steady force; one that can weather any external storm. By nurturing this core, you ensure you stay rooted even when challenges shake your resolve.

A Unique Moment of Standing My Ground

A recent experience at my grandson's birthday party challenged my ability to hold my ground. The cake had arrived late, and when we finally opened the box, it looked nothing like what we'd ordered. The design was sloppy, and the colors were completely wrong. Everyone was upset, especially my daughter, who had spent weeks planning the party. As the frustration bubbled over, I noticed everyone glancing at me, as if I had some magical solution—or worse, as if I was somehow responsible.

My instinct was to apologize. It was a reflex I'd relied on for years to calm tense situations, even when I had nothing to do with the problem. But I stopped myself. Instead, I took a deep breath and said, "This isn't what we were expecting, but we can make the best of it. Let's focus on making the day special for him—he won't even notice the cake isn't perfect."

The room went quiet for a moment, and then my daughter sighed and nodded. "You're right," she said. "He's just going to remember having fun, not the cake."

And just like that, the energy shifted. Instead of stressing over the cake, everyone rallied around my grandson, making sure his day was filled with laughter and joy. This moment reinforced how important it is to set boundaries and stay grounded. For the first time, I realized how powerful it was to offer calm and encouragement without taking on guilt or blame that didn't belong to me. It wasn't my responsibility to fix everything, and that simple shift allowed me to enjoy the celebration fully—without the weight of unnecessary apologies.

Living by Your Values

When we stray from our core values, life often feels unbalanced. Stress and frustration creep in because our actions aren't aligned with what truly matters to us. Identifying and living by your values helps you make decisions with clarity and confidence, creating a life rooted in authenticity.

For me, my values include honesty, balance, and creativity. These principles guide my decisions—from how I approach my work to the way I show up in relationships. They function as my compass, reminding me to honor what matters most even when the winds of expectation blow strongly.

Brené Brown, in her book *Daring Greatly*, emphasizes the importance of aligning actions with values. She describes how this alignment creates a sense of purpose and authenticity and strengthens our ability to remain steadfast even when external pressures challenge us.

Reflect on what values guide your life. What principles feel non-negotiable to you? For instance, living by my value of balance has positively impacted my relationships. By carving out time for family amidst a busy schedule, I've strengthened those connections while honoring my own well-being. When your decisions reflect these values, you create a life that feels true and enriching.

What are the values you hold most dear, and how do they shape your daily decisions? How might living in alignment with those values create clarity and freedom in your life?

Aligning with your values doesn't just bring clarity; it creates freedom. When you are firmly rooted in what matters most to you, it becomes easier to say no to things that don't align. The guilt lessens, the doubts fade, and your choices feel lighter because they reflect who you truly are. This isn't just a personal victory—it's a shift that positively impacts how you interact with the world around you.

Illustration:
The Wind and the Kite

Inner strength is the string that holds a kite steady. The wind—external expectations and challenges—gives the kite flight but can also send it spiraling if unchecked.

The string provides clarity, calm, and control—The Three C's—to guide the kite's path, even when the wind becomes turbulent.

Like a kite steadied by its string, leaders like Nelson Mandela have shown how inner strength can guide us through turbulent winds, inspiring us to navigate challenges with resilience. Imprisoned for twenty-seven years for opposing apartheid, Mandela endured extreme hardship, yet he emerged not with bitterness but with a deep sense of purpose and unwavering conviction. His ability to remain steadfast, foster reconciliation, and lead South Africa through a historic transition demonstrated the power of inner strength in overcoming adversity. His story reminds us that resilience isn't about avoiding the storm—it's about learning to navigate it with wisdom and courage.

When we firmly hold on to our "string," we can navigate life's winds with resilience, soaring to new heights without losing our sense of self. Much like a kite's string provides stability amidst turbulence, The Three C's anchor us, guiding our choices no matter the challenges.

Temptation and Consistency: The Real Test of Strength

Making the decision to prioritize yourself is just the beginning. The challenge lies in following through when the world tempts you to revert back.

Strength is not about being unshakable, it's about the willingness to realign with your values when the temptation to please others resurfaces. The struggle to stay true to your values amidst external pressures is universal. True strength lies in embracing vulnerability as a cornerstone of resilience—an idea many experts, including Brené Brown, advocate. Vulnerability doesn't weaken us; it allows us to stay open to growth and aligned with our goals.

Consider this diet analogy: Progress isn't lost because of one cheat meal; the real challenge arises when a single slip spirals into repeated choices that stray from your goals. Like building a healthier lifestyle, cultivating inner strength isn't about perfection. It's about recognizing missteps as opportunities to realign with your goals. True strength is found in recognizing the misstep and quickly getting back on track.

For instance, after saying no to overcommitting in one area of my life, I found myself questioning my choice days later. The familiar urge to "make up for it" by overextending myself elsewhere crept in. But I reminded myself of the great goal: clarity, calm, and control. By staying rooted in my decision, I reinforced my resilience and proved to myself that honoring my limits wasn't a loss—it was a victory.

Choosing yourself requires courage and consistency—qualities that grow stronger with every decision to prioritize your peace and authenticity. Realigning after missteps isn't about avoiding mistakes but about turning them into steppingstones toward greater clarity and strength.

The Three Cs:
A Framework for Inner Strength

Inner strength thrives on clarity, calm, and control.

1. Clarity: This is the foundation of knowing what matters most. When you're clear on your values, it's easier to make decisions that align with your truth. For instance, consider someone navigating a difficult career choice. By focusing on their core values—such as personal growth and work-life balance—they can make a decision that feels true to themselves rather than succumbing to external pressures.

2. Calm: This is your ability to remain steady in the face of external pressure. Calm doesn't mean avoiding conflict; it means approaching challenges with intentionality rather than reaction. For example, during moments of stress, grounding techniques like taking deep breaths or pausing before responding can cultivate calm and intentionality. Imagine a team leader facing a tense meeting—by pausing and speaking with measured intention, they can defuse tension and guide the conversation effectively.

3. Control: This is about taking ownership of your choices and actions. While you can't control others' expectations, you can control how you respond

to them. Building control requires practice—resisting the urge to react impulsively and focusing instead on thoughtful responses. Picture someone receiving unexpected criticism; instead of reacting defensively, they take a moment to reflect and respond with clarity and poise.

Boundaries are not walls that separate us from others but bridges that protect and honor our well-being. They allow us to create space for what truly matters while maintaining healthy relationships. For example, setting boundaries in a professional environment might mean declining additional tasks when you're already at capacity. This decision not only protects your energy but also enhances your ability to focus on the tasks that align with your priorities.

When you integrate these Three C's into your daily life, they function as your anchor, keeping you steady even when external forces threaten to pull you off course. Having a solid foundation of clarity, calm, and control is essential, but boundaries are the structures that protect this foundation in our relationships.

The Importance of Boundaries

Theresa's story comes to mind. As a nurse, she found herself constantly saying "yes" to extra shifts and responsibilities, even when it left her drained. She worried that setting boundaries would make her seem unkind or uncommitted. But over time, she realized that her well-being wasn't just important—it was essential to being the nurse, mother, and friend she wanted to be.

This serves as a powerful reminder that boundaries are not selfish; they're acts of self-respect and empowerment. By creating space for her needs, Theresa not only regained her energy but also improved the quality of her care for others.

What areas of your life could benefit from clearer boundaries? How might setting them up improve both your well-being and your connections with others?

Mastering the Inner Dialogue

Our greatest battles often happen within. Self-doubt whispers that we're not enough. Perfectionism tells us we must do more. These voices can be loud, but they're not invincible.

Carlos, an IT specialist, once struggled with constant self-doubt at work. He worried about speaking up in meetings, fearing he'd be judged. But he decided to challenge those thoughts, reminding himself of his qualifications and the value he brought to the team. Slowly, he started contributing more and found that his colleagues respected his insights. Overcoming his inner battle allowed Carlos to step into his confidence and thrive in his role.

Resilience starts with self-compassion, being kind to yourself even when you falter. When doubt creeps in, ask yourself: What would I say to a dear friend in this situation? Chances are, you'd offer understanding and encouragement. Give yourself that same grace. How can you show yourself compassion the next time you face self-doubt? Reflect on a recent moment when you needed kindness and consider how extending grace to yourself might have changed the outcome.

A Foundation to Build On

Inner strength isn't something we're born with; it's something we cultivate through choices, experiences, and intentional care. Each moment you choose to honor your needs, each time you set a boundary, you are building a foundation that will support you through life's storms. Every decision to prioritize yourself, no matter how small, builds this foundation brick by brick, creating a resilient and meaningful life.

You don't have to be unshakable to be strong. Strength lies in your willingness to grow, adapt, and stand firm in your truth. Trust in the resilience you've already built and the strength that will continue to grow with you. As you move forward, take one small step today to honor your values or set a boundary. These actions, though small, lay the groundwork for a deeply satisfying life that is aligned with your values.

CHAPTER SIX:

EMPOWERING RELATIONSHIP DYNAMICS

> " *The most common way people give up their power is by thinking they don't have any.* —*Alice Walker* "

---

*H*ave you ever left a conversation feeling unheard, wondering why your voice always seems to be the quietest in the room? Maybe you've stayed silent to avoid conflict or let someone else's needs overshadow your own. These moments can leave us questioning our worth, but they also hold a chance to rediscover our voice and reclaim our power.

Owning Your Voice

Empowerment doesn't mean overpowering someone else. It's about standing in your truth with confidence and grace, while asserting your needs without guilt or fear. However, it's important to acknowledge the challenges this can bring, such as fear of rejection or resistance from others. For instance, you might worry about how a friend will react if you set a boundary, or you might face pushbacks in a workplace setting. Recognizing these potential hurdles helps you prepare and persevere in honoring your voice.

For instance, imagine a scenario where you're in a team meeting, and your ideas are being overlooked. Standing in your truth might mean calmly interjecting with, "I'd like to add my perspective here," ensuring your contribution is heard. Or in a personal relationship, it could mean expressing, "I need time for myself this weekend to recharge," when you feel stretched too thin. By making these small yet powerful decisions, you reinforce your worth and invite others to respect your boundaries. These actions prove confidence without compromising respect for others. Reclaiming your voice is a journey that requires both courage and consistency.

Rediscovering your voice doesn't happen overnight, but each step you take builds momentum toward a life where you feel heard, valued, and respected. It's about progress, not perfection, each effort plants a seed for growth.

Recognizing Relationship Imbalances

Picture this: A group of friends plan a weekend trip, and you're the one who ends up organizing everything—from booking the hotel to coordinating schedules. By the time the trip begins, you're too exhausted to enjoy it because all the emotional and logistical labor has fallen on you. Sound familiar?

This might seem like a harmless scenario, but it highlights a deeper issue: imbalance. Relationships thrive on shared responsibilities and mutual respect, but when one person consistently carries more weight—whether through expectations, decision-making, or emotional labor—the dynamic becomes strained. Emotional labor, for instance, involves the often-invisible effort of managing others' emotions, such as mediating conflicts, remembering important dates, or providing constant reassurance. These hidden efforts often go unnoticed, yet they are pivotal to keeping harmony in relationships.

To address this, you can start by openly discussing the distribution of responsibilities within your relationships. For example, if you find yourself always planning family events, propose a shared schedule or rotate tasks to ensure everyone contributes. Additionally, acknowledging and appreciating the effort involved in emotional labor helps confirm its importance and encourages mutual support. This hidden work can be exhausting and, when unacknowledged, contributes to imbalances that strain relationships.

Think about your own relationships. Are there areas where you feel you're carrying more than your fair share? Recognizing these imbalances is the first step toward change. When you take the time to reflect on these dynamics, you empower yourself to advocate healthier interactions.

Restoring Balance in Relationships

Visualize a set of scales representing influence and respect within a relationship. When these scales tilt too far in one direction, the imbalance creates tension. Our goal is to restore equilibrium by redefining how power runs between you and the people in your life.

One way to do this is by setting boundaries. Boundaries are not barriers; they are bridges connecting you to others in ways that protect your well-being. By defining where your needs begin and end, boundaries create space for mutual respect and collaboration.

Consider Julia, a caregiver for her aging parents who felt overwhelmed by her siblings' lack of involvement. Instead of continuing to shoulder everything alone, she set clear boundaries during a family meeting, saying, "I need help managing Mom's appointments. Let's divide responsibilities." Julia's boundary wasn't a rejection; it was an invitation for collaboration.

Boundaries are not just about saying "no." They are about saying "yes" to a healthier version of yourself and your relationships. For instance, setting boundaries might look like carving out specific time each week for self-care or asking a friend to respect your need for quiet time during a stressful period. It could also mean agreeing to limits on work-related calls after hours or being upfront about financial expectations in shared expenses. Boundaries create clarity, reduce resentment, and allow relationships to flourish authentically. Julia's story shows how boundaries invite respect and mutual growth, rather than division.

Communicating with Clarity

Clarity in communication transforms dynamics. It promotes understanding, reduces tension, and ensures your voice is heard. Using "I" statements helps frame conversations around your experience rather than placing blame:

- Instead of: "You never listen to me."

- Try: "I feel unheard when I share my thoughts, and I'd appreciate more space to express myself."

Clear communication prevents misunderstandings and ensures others respect their needs. Without clarity, miscommunication can entangle relationships in a web of frustration, perpetuating imbalances.

Marshall Rosenberg's *Nonviolent Communication* emphasizes finding and expressing needs without judgment. For example, observing without evaluating can be applied in family settings by describing an issue factually, such as saying, "The dishes have been in the sink for two days," rather than assigning blame with, "You never do the dishes." In workplace settings, this could look like stating, "The project deadline has been moved up," instead of, "You didn't give us enough notice about the change." These approaches create a neutral starting point for discussion and reduce defensiveness.

Two key principles of this framework include observing without evaluating and expressing feelings and needs directly to encourage understanding. For example, instead of saying, "You're always late," you might say, "I feel frustrated when our meetings start late because I value punctuality." Rosenberg writes, "When we understand the needs that motivate our own and others' behavior, we have no enemies." Practicing this framework creates opportunities for connection rather than conflict.

Building Respect in Relationships

Mutual respect is the foundation of healthy connections, and it can be **strengthened** by practicing these habits:

- **Active Listening**: Fully engage during conversations by listening without interrupting, reflecting back what you hear, and asking clarifying questions to show you understand. For example, try saying, *"I hear that you're feeling overwhelmed by the situation; would you like to talk through it?"* This deepens trust and ensures others feel heard.

- **Appreciation**: Regularly express gratitude, both verbally and through small gestures. Acknowledge efforts with comments like, *"Your feedback made such a difference in this project; thank you for your insight."* Even small actions like leaving a kind note or a quick text can make someone feel valued.

- **Mutual Support**: Build collaboration by sharing responsibilities and celebrating successes together. Ask how you can help, such as saying, *"What's one thing I can do to make this easier for you?"* Emotional support matters, too; being present during tough times and cheering for milestones strengthens bonds.

Imagine two friends working on a shared project. One listens intently as the other shares their ideas, offering constructive feedback with statements like, *"That's a great concept! What if we also included this angle to expand on it further?"* This active listening not only validates the speaker's input but also builds a sense of shared ownership in the project. Meanwhile, the second friend takes time to express gratitude, saying, *"I really appreciate how you always bring such creative energy to our discussions. It inspires me to think bigger."* This exchange reinforces their bond, showing that each contribution is valued.

Their collaboration thrives because both friends prioritize intentional actions. Through active listening, they create an open and supportive environment where ideas flow freely without fear of judgment. By expressing appreciation, they maintain a positive and motivating atmosphere. These seemingly small behaviors, when practiced consistently, lead to a partnership where mutual respect and understanding serve as the foundation for success. Together, they demonstrate that meaningful connections grow stronger when effort is made to recognize and honor each other's strengths and contributions.

Rediscovering Your Inner Power

Take a moment to consider the relationships in your life. Reflect on the following questions:

Where do you feel empowered? Why? Think about moments when your contributions are acknowledged, your opinions are valued, and your boundaries are respected. For instance, do you feel most empowered in relationships where there's open communication and mutual appreciation? Pinpointing these dynamics can help you identify what makes you feel strong and supported.

Which dynamics leave you feeling diminished? What changes might help? Consider situations where your voice is overlooked, or your efforts go unacknowledged. What patterns do you notice? Is it a lack of communication, an imbalance in responsibilities, or unspoken expectations? Reflecting on these questions can illuminate areas where change is needed to restore balance.

Turn Reflection into Action: Writing down your thoughts can help you clarify patterns and track progress. For example, create a journal or use a reflection worksheet to note specific situations, feelings, and potential solutions. Over time, revisiting your notes will reveal how your relationships and sense of self evolve, providing motivation to keep advocating for positive change.

Practical Steps to Reclaim Power:

1. **Start Small:** Begin by identifying one area where you'd like to feel more empowered. This could be speaking up in meetings, setting boundaries in a personal relationship, or asking for help when you need it.

2. **Set Intentions:** Write down clear, actionable goals. For example, "I will express my thoughts in at least one meeting this week," or "I will have a conversation with my friend about sharing responsibilities."

3. **Practice Self-Awareness:** Pay attention to how you feel in different interactions. Do you leave certain conversations feeling lighter and others feeling drained? Use this awareness to guide your decisions and focus on relationships that uplift you.

4. **Celebrate Progress:** Acknowledge even small wins. If you set a boundary, spoke up for yourself, or expressed your needs, take a moment to recognize your effort and courage.

5. **Visualization for Empowerment:** Imagine your ideal relationships. What do they look like? How do you feel when interacting with others who value and respect you? This visualization can serve as a reminder of what you're working toward and inspire you to continue advocating for your needs.

Real-Life Lessons in Reclaiming Balance

Brian, an educator, often felt burdened by the societal expectations of being the "provider" in his family. This role, traditionally tied to financial stability, came with unspoken pressures that left little room for his personal goals or passions. He found himself caught in a cycle of overwork, neglecting his own well-being to fulfill what he believed were his family's expectations.

The Breaking Point

One evening, during a discussion about work-life balance with close friends, Brian shared his exhaustion and his long-suppressed dream of starting a community outreach program. For years, he had pushed this passion aside, believing it was impractical or selfish to pursue. Speaking his truth felt risky—what if his family saw this as neglecting his responsibilities? Yet, to his surprise, his vulnerability was met with encouragement rather than criticism. His family and peers recognized his desire not as a departure from his duties but as an extension of who he was.

Redefining "Provider"

Brian began to rethink what "providing" meant. It wasn't solely about financial contributions; it was also about being emotionally present and leading a life of fulfillment and authenticity. By pursuing his dream, Brian found himself more energized and emotionally available for his family; ultimately, strengthening their connection. He realized that when he nurtured his own passions, he could show up as his best self for those he cared about.

Practical Takeaways for Readers Brian's journey offers valuable lessons for anyone struggling with similar pressures:

1. **Challenge Societal Norms:** Reflect on the roles or labels you feel obligated to fulfill. Are they serving your happiness, or are they rooted in external expectations? Rewriting these narratives can create space for personal growth.

2. **Speak Your Truth:** Vulnerability can be powerful. Opening up about your feelings, even when it feels uncomfortable, can lead to unexpected support and understanding from others.

3. **Align Your Goals:** Consider how pursuing your passions might enhance your ability to support loved ones. When you lead with authenticity, you model a life of purpose and joy for those around you.

4. **Start Small:** If you feel overwhelmed by the idea of making a big life change, begin with manageable steps. For Brian, this meant dedicating just a few hours each week to planning his outreach program while maintaining his other responsibilities.

A Life of Balance and Purpose

Brian's story highlights an important truth. Balance isn't about perfection; it's about honoring both your commitments and your dreams. By redefining what it means to provide, he reclaimed his voice and forged a path that allowed him to lead with authenticity and renewed purpose. His journey is a reminder that prioritizing your needs isn't selfish, it's a vital step toward creating a fulfilling, meaningful life.

Overcoming Fear and Guilt in Relationships

To break the cycle of imbalance caused by prioritizing others' needs at the expense of your own, it's essential to confront the discomfort of standing your ground. For instance, you might find yourself always agreeing to plans or tasks to avoid conflict, even when they stretch you beyond your capacity. Over time, this silent compromise erodes your sense of self-worth and strains the relationship.

When you avoid expressing your needs, it inadvertently communicates that they don't matter. This lack of expression can also make you feel powerless and reinforce the idea that your voice doesn't carry weight. On the other hand, standing your ground—even if it feels uncomfortable—signals that your voice and boundaries are equally important. Standing firm could mean declining a request for your time when you're already stretched thin or voicing your opinion in a group setting where you typically stay silent.

Shifting Your Mindset

Conflict doesn't have to be destructive. When approached with care, it can deepen mutual understanding and respect. View disagreements as opportunities to encourage growth rather than as battles to win or avoid. Imagine a disagreement with a colleague. Instead of avoiding the topic to keep the peace, consider saying, "I respect your point of view, but I'd like to share my perspective, too." This small shift builds mutual respect while honoring your voice.

Embracing Your Worth

Guilt often whispers that prioritizing yourself is selfish, but the opposite is true. Prioritizing yourself leads to better outcomes in relationships by allowing you to bring your best self to the table. When you take time to recharge and honor your needs, you can engage more fully and effectively with others, building stronger connections and mutual respect. It also promotes personal well-being, enabling you to maintain emotional balance and resilience in the face of challenges. When you respect your needs, you empower others to do the same.

Healthy relationships thrive on mutual respect and shared responsibility. Addressing these patterns fosters long-term connection and deeper understanding. By asserting your needs, you strengthen both your sense of self and the foundation of the relationship.

Script for Boundary-Setting Conversations

1. **Start with an observation:** Begin the conversation by neutrally stating the situation. For example, "I've noticed that I am managing most of the household tasks lately."

2. **Express your feelings:** Use "I" statements to communicate how the situation affects you. "I'm feeling overwhelmed and would really appreciate some help."

3. **State your need clearly:** Clearly articulate your boundary or request. "I need us to divide these tasks more evenly so that it's manageable for everyone."

4. **Invite collaboration:** Encourage the other person to engage in the solution. "How do you feel about us setting up a schedule to share the responsibilities?"

Coach's Example in Action:

Imagine you're overwhelmed by a colleague always assigning last-minute tasks. You could say: "I've noticed that a lot of tasks come to me at the last minute. I've been feeling stressed because it leaves me with very little time to manage my workload effectively. Going forward, I'd appreciate receiving tasks with at least two days' notice. How can we work together to make this happen?"

Practicing scripts like this helps build confidence and demonstrates that setting boundaries is not about conflict but about promoting respect and balance. The more you practice these conversations, the more natural they will feel, empowering you to advocate for yourself effectively.

Small Steps to Stronger Relationships

Change happens incrementally. Start by identifying one relationship or dynamic in your life where the scales feel unbalanced. Perhaps it's a friendship where you give more than you receive or a workplace interaction where your ideas aren't valued. Choose one action—expressing your feelings, setting a boundary, or simply reclaiming your balance.

Remember, small shifts build momentum. Each choice to honor your needs reinforces your ability to create healthier, more fulfilling relationships. Each step you take is a testament to your strength and a move toward deeper connections.

Closing Thoughts: Looking Ahead

Balanced relationships start with empowering yourself. When you reclaim your voice and honor your needs, you inspire others to do the same. Take one small step today—whether it's setting a boundary, expressing your feelings, or taking time for self-care—and begin building the foundation for healthier, more balanced relationships. This creates space for growth, connection, and mutual respect.

This chapter isn't the end of your journey; it's the beginning. Next, we'll take the strength you've built and explore how to create a life of purpose and joy, empowering you to live authentically and thrive.

PART III:
EMBRACING GROWTH

CHAPTER SEVEN:

LIVING LIBERATED

> 66
> *Freedom is not the absence of commitments, but the ability to choose—and commit myself to— what is best for me.—**Paulo Coelho***
> 99

---

*I*f someone asked you to describe what it means to live authentically, how would you answer? Chances are, you might pause, uncertain. The truth is, many of us have never been asked that question—not by others and not by ourselves.

We've been handed scripts by society, dictating what's expected and acceptable. But what if those scripts don't reflect who you truly are or want to be?

Living liberated is about rewriting that script that serves you, is consistent with your values, and allows you to live authentically. Living authentically means embracing your unique identity, making choices rooted in your core values, and letting go of roles that feel imposed rather than chosen. Living authentically is reflected in small choices—speaking up, prioritizing joy, or saying no to draining commitments. These steps align your life with your true self.

When you live authentically, it strengthens relationships by fostering honesty and mutual respect. It also transforms career satisfaction, allowing you to pursue paths that resonate deeply with your passions and skills, rather than those dictated by external pressures. For example, it might look like prioritizing a career that aligns with your passions rather than societal expectations or setting boundaries in a friendship where your needs often go unheard. To start identifying these areas, consider moments in your life where you feel a disconnect between your actions and your true desires. Reflecting on these experiences can help you uncover opportunities for realignment. It's about taking steps that reflect your true self, even if they challenge conventional norms. It's about aligning your external life with your inner truth. It's not about what the world says you should be; it's about embracing the freedom to define your life on your terms.

A Personal Turning Point

There was a time when I felt disconnected from myself, as though I was living someone else's script. My decisions, whether about my career, relationships, or hobbies, reflected expectations I had internalized, not desires that resonated with my heart. The disconnect left me drained and restless.

One evening, while reflecting on a strained friendship, I replayed a conversation where I felt dismissed. It had been a casual chat, or at least it started that way. I had hesitated before bringing up something deeply personal that had been weighing on me for months. When I finally found the courage to speak, the response was a wave of indifference.

"Honestly," they said with a shrug, "I think you're overreacting."

The words hit me like a dull thud, but it wasn't just the words, it was the tone. The kind of dismissiveness that makes you feel small and foolish for even trying to open up. I remember the way they glanced at their phone, their attention already somewhere else, as if my vulnerability was a distraction.

I tried to laugh it off, telling myself I was being too sensitive. But replaying the scene, I realized this wasn't an isolated moment—it was part of a pattern where I allowed others to dismiss my feelings, leaving me questioning my worth. That night, I dreamed of my late mother. She appeared calm, her words gentle yet piercing: "The greatest love of all is learning to love yourself."

Her message stayed with me, lingering like a song I couldn't get out of my head. In the stillness of that dream, her words felt like an invitation—an urgent call to step back from the roles and relationships that had tethered me to a life that didn't feel like my own.

The next morning, I sat with a journal and started to write. What do I need? What do I want? What am I willing to let go of to reclaim myself? The answers didn't come all at once, but the act of asking those questions began a journey of rediscovery.

It was time to prioritize my needs, step back from draining connections, and start exploring what truly mattered to me. Over the next few months, I made difficult but necessary changes—letting go of relationships and roles that no longer served me. Each decision bringing me closer to a life that felt genuinely mine.

These changes weren't easy, but they were transformative. Each step I took was a declaration of self-worth—a reminder that I deserved a life that felt aligned with my values and passions. Through this journey, I began to see the power of small, consistent changes and their profound impact on my overall sense of peace and purpose.

This book you're holding is a result of that journey. Writing became a liberating act for me to reclaim my voice and chart my path. Looking back, I see those challenges not as barriers but as opportunities to gain experience stronger and more aligned with my truth.

If I hadn't embraced the tools and steps I describe here, this book wouldn't exist. And now, as you hold it in your hands, I hope it offers you the same clarity and courage to chart your own path toward a life that feels authentically yours.

The Practice of Liberation

Living free from the weight of expectations means aligning your choices with your values and desires. It requires shedding the masks we wear to fit into roles others impose.

Hakim's story exemplifies this. As a social worker, he believed his worth came from his tireless service to others. But, constantly saying "yes" to requests left him depleted. A conversation with a colleague shifted his perspective. She reminded him that self-care wasn't selfish, it was essential.

Hakim began making small but impactful changes. He started by establishing clear boundaries with clients and colleagues, ensuring he wasn't overextending himself. He scheduled regular moments of rest and reflection, allowing him to recharge without guilt. He also incorporated mindfulness practices and set aside time for activities that brought him joy.

By setting boundaries and prioritizing self-care, Hakim felt more energized and effective. His contributions didn't lessen; they deepened as he regained fulfillment and focus. Over time, he realized that caring for himself allowed him to be even more present in his work.

Hakim's journey teaches that when we create space for ourselves, we can serve others more meaningfully. After making these adjustments, Hakim noticed that his relationships grew stronger because he was more present and attentive. Professionally, he found that his renewed energy and focus enabled him to provide better support to his clients while maintaining a sense of fulfillment in his work.

Removing Barriers

Living true to yourself means letting go of misaligned roles and beliefs, like societal pressures or the idea that self-sacrifice equals virtue.

You might notice these barriers when you feel persistent dissatisfaction or resentment in certain areas of your life. Take a few moments to journal about a recent experience where these emotions surfaced. Reflect on what triggered these feelings and consider whether they point to expectations or roles that no longer serve you. For instance, staying in a job or relationship out of obligation rather than desire can be a sign. Paying attention to these emotions can help identify the areas where change is needed.

A person might stay in a job they dislike in order to meet societal expectations, or a caregiver might neglect self-care, believing it's selfish.

These scenarios show how societal and internal pressures can prevent individuals from living authentically. Recognizing these barriers is the first step to moving beyond them.

For me, reconnecting with my creative passions was a turning point. Writing, something I had dismissed as frivolous, became a way to express my voice and find joy. It reminded me that reclaiming ourselves isn't about loss; it's about making room for what matters.

Think of what passions or pursuits you've been putting off. Maybe it's picking up a paintbrush, exploring a hobby you've dismissed as impractical, or setting aside time to reconnect with nature. What would it feel like to let these joys take center stage in your life?

Cultivating Joy

Living with purpose brings joy—not because life becomes perfect but because it feels deeply rooted in what truly matters. Joy comes from simple, intentional actions, like sharing a laugh with a loved one, creating something meaningful, or taking a quiet moment to appreciate your progress. To uncover your own sources of joy, try this quick exercise: List three activities or moments from the past week that brought you a sense of peace or happiness. Reflect on what made these moments special and consider how you can intentionally incorporate similar actions into your daily life. To identify these moments in your own life, think about what activities leave you feeling energized or at peace. Reflect on past moments of joy, whether it's a creative project you lost yourself in, a heartfelt conversation, or even a peaceful walk in nature. These clues can guide you toward the small, meaningful actions that nurture joy. This joy is nurtured through the people, activities, and pursuits that uplift and inspire us.

For Hakim, it meant dedicating a weekend each month to self-care. For me, it was embracing creativity and reconnecting with passions I had long suppressed.

Joy also comes from celebrating progress. Each step, no matter how small, is part of the larger journey toward self-discovery and fulfillment.

The Weeding Process:
A Guide to Living Liberated

Imagine your life as a garden. Over time, weeds—representing societal pressures, self-doubt, fears, and misaligned commitments—can crowd out the flowers you planted long ago. The flowers represent your authentic passions, values, and dreams. The process of "Weeding the Garden" is about clearing space for these blooms to thrive and creating a life aligned with your true self.

Liberation doesn't mean starting over; it means nurturing what's already there and removing what no longer serves you. Whether personally, professionally, or within your family, this step-by-step framework will guide you to cultivate a flourishing garden that is unique to your life.

Sarah's Story

Sarah's life was packed with commitments, but none of them felt like her own. Her boss constantly assigned her extra work, her friends expected her to always be available, and her family relied on her to manage their problems. Somewhere along the way, she had stopped prioritizing herself. She hadn't taken a real break in years, yet she couldn't shake the guilt at the thought of saying no. She believed that being busy equated to being valuable and that declining requests would make her seem selfish.

One day, after another exhausting week of catering to everyone else's needs, Sarah finally asked herself: *What about me?* She realized she had been living on autopilot, tending to everyone else's priorities while neglecting her own. Something had to change.

Sarah began by identifying the areas in her life that left her feeling drained. She recognized that she was overcommitted at work and constantly saying yes to projects she didn't want. She saw how her social life had become an obligation rather than a source of joy. And she acknowledged that her role as the family peacemaker had taken a toll on her emotional well-being. These were the weeds in her garden, and if she wanted to create space for herself, she needed to pull them out.

Next, she examined the roots of these weeds. Why had she allowed them to grow? She discovered that her inability to say no stemmed from a deep-seated desire to be liked and validated. The belief that she needed to stay busy to be worthy had shaped her decisions for years.

Determined to reclaim her time, Sarah started small. She set boundaries by declining extra projects at work. She reserved one evening a week for herself—what she called "Sarah's time"—where she could rest without guilt. And instead of always taking on family conflicts, she let others step in.

With newfound clarity, Sarah began planting new seeds in her life. She reconnected with her love of painting, signing up for a class she had once abandoned. She also scheduled monthly lunches with a friend who uplifted her, prioritizing relationships that fueled her rather than drained her.

As she tended to her new commitments, Sarah realized that self-care wasn't selfish, it was necessary. She started a habit of checking in with herself every Sunday and reflecting on what was working and adjusting where needed. She saw that while weeds could always grow back, maintaining her garden was an ongoing process; one that required intention and care.

Step 1: Identify the Weeds

What it means: Reflect on areas in your life that feel draining, unfulfilling, or misaligned with your values. These are the "weeds" choking your garden.

Workshop Exercise:

- Take five minutes to journal your responses to the following prompts:
  - Where do I feel stuck or unhappy in my life?
  - What roles or commitments feel like obligations rather than choices?
  - Are there relationships that leave me feeling drained or unsupported?

Example:

- *Personal:* "I keep saying yes to social events I don't enjoy because I feel guilty declining."

- *Professional:* "I'm staying in a career that pays well but doesn't align with my passion for teaching."

- *Familial:* "I've taken on the role of always solving family conflicts, and it's wearing me out."

Step 2: Examine the Roots

What it means: Explore the societal, family, or personal beliefs that sustain these weeds. Ask yourself why you've allowed them to grow.

Workshop Exercise:

- Reflect on these questions:
    - What beliefs or fears keep me from removing these "weeds?"
    - Am I holding onto guilt, fear of judgment, or the need for external validation?
    - What would happen if I let go of these roles or expectations?

Example:

- *Personal:* "I feel like saying no to social events will make people think I'm selfish."

- *Professional:* "I'm afraid leaving this job will disappoint my parents, who value financial stability."

- *Familial:* "If I stop managing family conflicts, I worry my family will fall apart."

Step 3: Choose Your Tools

What it means: Decide what actions will help you remove the weeds and take control of your garden. This could involve setting boundaries, exploring new opportunities, or seeking support.

Workshop Exercise:

- Write down one action you could take for each "weed" you identified. Use this template:
    - The weed is: _____.
    - My first step is: _____.

Example:

- *Personal:* "The weed is attending every social event. My first step is politely declining one invitation this month."

- *Professional:* "The weed is staying in an unfulfilling career. My first step is enrolling in an online teaching certification."

- *Familial:* "The weed is taking on every family problem. My first step is letting a sibling manage the next family disagreement.

Step 4: Plant New Seeds

What it means: Introduce passions, activities, or commitments that align with your values and bring joy. These are the new seeds that will grow into vibrant flowers in your garden.

Workshop Exercise:

- Reflect on the following:
  - What activities make me lose track of time?
  - What hobbies, interests, or dreams have I been putting off?
  - How can I incorporate small moments of joy into my daily routine?

Example:

- *Personal:* "I'll start a yoga class on weekends to reconnect with my body."

- *Professional:* "I'll use my vacation days to attend a teaching workshop."

- *Familial:* "I'll suggest a family game night to bring us closer in a way that feels light and fun."

Step 5: Tend the Garden

What it means: Regularly reflect and adjust to ensure your garden stays vibrant. Weeds may grow back, but consistent care will keep your life aligned with your values.

Workshop Exercise:

- Set a recurring "garden check-in":
  - What's thriving in my life right now?
  - What's feeling out of balance or draining me?
  - Are there new "weeds" I need to address?

Example:

- *Personal:* "I'll journal weekly about what brought me joy and what felt stressful."

- *Professional:* "I'll reassess my workload each quarter to make sure I'm not taking on too much."

- *Familial:* "I'll have monthly check-ins with my family to set expectations and share responsibilities."

Your Flourishing Garden: Moving Forward

Living free of external control is an ongoing process. It requires regular reflection and the courage to make changes as you grow. Just like tending a garden, your flourishing life depends on consistent care and attention.

Ask yourself:

- Are my choices aligned with my values?

- What can I release to make room for what matters?

- How can I nurture my passions and priorities today?

Takeaway Exercise: Write a personal "garden vision." Picture how you want your life to look and feel in six months if you remove the weeds, plant new seeds, and tend to your garden. What will your relationships, career, and personal time reflect? How will your life feel when you are truly liberated?

Your journey to freedom is ongoing, but with each intentional action, you cultivate a life that is vibrant, balanced, and uniquely yours. As you tend to your inner garden, remember that the process itself is just as meaningful as the results. Each moment of care—whether it's reflecting, taking a small step, or celebrating progress—is a declaration of self-worth and growth.

With care, courage, and commitment, your garden is waiting to bloom. The choice to begin is yours.

Author Spotlight:
Martha Beck and *The Way of Integrity*

Martha Beck's work on rediscovering authenticity offers a powerful lens for understanding what it means to live liberated. In her book, *The Way of Integrity: Finding the Path to Your True Self*, Beck writes, "Integrity is the cure for unhappiness. Period."

Her insights align perfectly with the themes of this chapter. Living liberated requires the courage to shed societal expectations and embrace a life designed around your own values and desires. Beck reminds us that when we align our lives with our true selves, we unlock a profound sense of freedom and fulfillment.

Closing Thoughts:
Anchored in Freedom

Reclaiming your voice and living authentically transforms every part of your life. By clearing external expectations, you nurture your passions and values.

The fact that you're holding this book is proof of what living liberated can look like—a tangible representation of rewriting the script to reflect your truth. Take five minutes today to reflect on one area of your life where you feel constrained and imagine one step you could take to make it more aligned with your values.

Of course, the journey won't always be smooth. Setbacks are inevitable, but they don't have to derail you. With care, courage, and love, you have the power to stay rooted in your authenticity—even when life pulls you in unexpected directions.

Your garden is waiting to bloom. And as you move forward, resilience will be your greatest tool for continuing to thrive.

CHAPTER **EIGHT:**

WHEN THE ROPE PULLS YOU BACK

> *You may encounter many defeats, but you must not be defeated. In fact, it may be necessary to encounter the defeats, so you can know who you are, what you can rise from, how you can still come out of it."—*
> ***Maya Angelou***

What's the moment when you feel pulled back? Is it answering that call or text from an ex who no longer values you? Is it the guilt that compels you to return to toxic environments because you're afraid of being called "brand new?" Or is it the pressure to solve everyone else's problems while ignoring the fire burning within your own home?

Setbacks often disguise themselves as comfort zones or unresolved ties that beckon us back. Comfort zones might look like familiar but unproductive routines, such as staying in a job that no longer fulfills you or maintaining relationships out of habit rather than genuine connection. These patterns, while seemingly safe, can keep you from moving forward. These are the moments when we question our progress and feel tempted to revert to old habits or relationships. But setbacks don't define us—they challenge us to grow, teaching us resilience and revealing the strength to honor who we are becoming.

Recognizing Setbacks as Part of the Journey

Challenges arise in many forms—personal challenges, professional disappointments, or internal struggles with doubt and fear. They're not signs of failure but natural parts of growth. When we view setbacks as opportunities to reflect, recalibrate, and learn, we can respond with acceptance rather than discouragement.

Think of setbacks as a teacher rather than an enemy. They don't block your path; they help shape it.

David's story illustrates this well. After spending months preparing for a promotion, David was passed over. Initially, he questioned his abilities, feeling disheartened. But instead of letting the setback define him, David sought feedback, identified growth opportunities, and honed his skills. When another opportunity came, he was more prepared than ever and succeeded.

Setbacks like David's are steppingstones toward resilience. They challenge us to pause, reflect, and recalibrate. When faced with a setback, ask yourself: What can I learn from this experience? How can this challenge prepare me for future opportunities? For example, consider someone who was overlooked for a promotion. By reflecting on the feedback received, they might identify skills to improve or better ways to highlight their contributions, turning the disappointment into a chance for professional growth. Shifting your focus from loss to growth helps reframe setbacks as valuable lessons.

- **Personal challenges:** Relationship struggles, health challenges, or emotional stress.

- **Professional obstacles:** Missed goals, career disappointments, or financial challenges.

- **Internal struggles:** Negative self-talk, self-doubt, or unresolved fears.

To address these barriers, try journaling about moments when these feelings surface.

Ask yourself: What triggered this thought? Is it based on fact or fear? For example, you might discover a recurring theme of self-doubt tied to a specific event, like a critical remark from a colleague. By identifying the trigger, you can challenge the thought and reframe it, such as focusing on your achievements instead of the critique. Recognizing and challenging patterns helps us build self-awareness and resilience, allowing us to face challenges with courage and view them as opportunities for growth rather than obstacles.

Building Resilience: The Foundation for Moving Forward

Resilience is our ability to adapt, recover, and grow stronger through adversity. Much like muscles that strengthen through resistance, resilience grows each time we encounter and overcome challenges.

To develop resilience in everyday life, consider the following steps:

- **Start with Self-Compassion**: Treat yourself with kindness during challenges, reframing them as lessons rather than failures. Self-compassion creates a safe space for growth, helping you acknowledge your emotions without judgment.

- **Focus on Small Wins**: Celebrate small victories to remind yourself of your capacity to progress, even in tough times. These incremental achievements serve as powerful reminders of your resilience.

- **Build a Support System**: Surround yourself with people who uplift and encourage you. Supportive connections can provide perspective, motivation, and a sense of belonging during tough times.

To bring these principles to life, I've developed a step-by-step Resilience Roadmap—a guide to help you navigate challenges, harness your inner strength, and transform setbacks into steppingstones toward growth.

The Resilience Roadmap: A Practical Guide

Step 1: Shift Your Mindset—Adopt a Growth Perspective

What it means: Challenges aren't obstacles; they're opportunities to learn. Embrace the idea that setbacks are steppingstones toward growth.

Brittany's story illustrates this perfectly. After a sudden breakup, Brittany leaned on friends, rediscovered activities she loved, and took small steps to rebuild her confidence. Rather than suppressing her pain, she reframed the breakup as a chance to reconnect with herself and explore what truly made her happy. This mindset shift allowed her to see the challenge as an opportunity for personal growth.

- **Practical Tip:** Recall a time when you overcame a challenge. How did that shape who you are today? Write down one lesson you learned from that experience.

Step 2:
Revisit Core Values – Define Your North Star

What it means: Ground yourself in what truly matters. Resilience grows when you align your actions with your values. Reflect on how overcoming challenges can benefit both you and those you care about.

- **Practical Tip:** Identify three core values (e.g., family, creativity, independence). Ask yourself: How does my resilience impact these values?

Step 3:
Build a Support System – Strength in Connection

What it means: Resilience flourishes in the company of supportive relationships. Surround yourself with people who encourage and uplift you.

- **Practical Tip:** List the people in your life who consistently support you. Reach out to express gratitude or ask for their input during challenging times.

Step 4:
Embrace Imperfection – Let Go of the Ideal

What it means: Release the pressure to succeed flawlessly. Embracing imperfection transforms setbacks into moments of growth rather than sources of shame.

- **Practical Tip:** Each time you face a setback, ask: "What's one thing I can learn from this?" Focus on progress, not perfection.

Step 5:
Develop Healthy Coping Mechanisms – Tend Your Inner Garden

What it means: Like a garden, resilience requires consistent care. Engage in practices that nurture your emotional well-being.

Sarah's approach demonstrates the power of healthy coping mechanisms. She started journaling about her feelings to process her emotions, signed up for a dance class she had always wanted to try, and began spending more time with people who valued her. These small but intentional actions nurtured her emotional well-being and helped her reclaim her sense of self.

- **Practical Tip:** Explore coping strategies such as journaling, meditating, exercising, or connecting with nature. Create a routine that supports your mental health.

Reflection reinforces the inner strength that often feels hidden during challenging times. By recalling your past victories and focusing on small, consistent actions, you create a foundation for resilience that supports you through life's uncertainties.

Turning Setbacks into Growth Opportunities

Obstacles often feel discouraging, but they hold immense potential for growth. Reflecting on what went wrong allows us to discover our triggers, learn about ourselves, and adjust for the future.

Considerations for Transforming Challenges:

- **Reflect:** Take stock of what happened and identify patterns.

- **Identify Lessons:** Learn about your strengths and areas for improvement.

- **Implement Changes:** Use these insights to prevent similar challenges and improve future outcomes.

For example, Ethan struggled after a business deal fell through. Initially, he blamed himself, replaying every decision and interaction in his mind, and wondering what he could have done differently. The self-doubt became overwhelming, making him hesitant to pursue new opportunities. He felt stuck, questioning his abilities and whether he was cut out for the business world.

After giving himself time to process the setback, Ethan decided to take a step back and analyze what went wrong. He realized that unclear communication had led to misaligned expectations with his client, creating a misunderstanding that ultimately derailed the deal. This insight was a turning point. Instead of dwelling on what he couldn't change, he began focusing on what he could improve.

Ethan invested in communication training, practiced delivering clear proposals, and set up regular check-ins with clients to ensure alignment throughout the process. These adjustments not only restored his confidence but also transformed his approach to business. When he landed his next partnership, it was with a client who valued his transparency and professionalism—qualities Ethan had worked hard to cultivate. Adjusting his approach not only helped Ethan recover but also positioned him to build stronger, more aligned partnerships in the future.

Letting Go of the Need for Perfection

Setbacks often challenge our perfectionistic tendencies, exposing the pressure we put on ourselves to succeed flawlessly. Embracing imperfection is a powerful step in turning setbacks into moments of growth, rather than sources of shame.

Strategies to Embrace Imperfection

- **Shift Your Perspective:** View setbacks as stepping-stones rather than roadblocks.

- **Focus on Progress, Not Perfection:** Celebrate each step forward, even if it's imperfect.

- **Challenge Negative Self-Talk:** When self-doubt arises, remind yourself that setbacks are a natural part of growth.

Leila often struggled with perfectionism—feeling paralyzed by the fear of failure. She grew up believing that mistakes equated to personal inadequacy, a belief that made her overanalyze every project she tackled. After missing a project deadline, she realized the pressure to be perfect was holding her back. By focusing on doing her best instead of achieving perfection, she began to enjoy her work more and found her productivity improved.

Stories of Resilience

Resilience takes many forms, and different people navigate their challenges in unique ways. The following stories illustrate how individuals from diverse backgrounds found ways to overcome obstacles and build stronger, more fulfilling lives.

Rafael's Story: After an unexpected layoff, Rafael felt uncertain about his future. Grieving the loss of his job, he initially felt stuck. But instead of letting the setback define him, he enrolled in online courses to upskill and pivoted himself into a career aligned with his passions. The layoff became a catalyst for reinvention.

Tanya's Story: Balancing motherhood and a demanding career, Tanya often felt overwhelmed by the weight of her responsibilities. After reaching a breaking point, she opened up to her family, sharing how she felt. With their support, she adjusted her routines, delegated some tasks, and prioritized self-care. Small, intentional changes helped her find balance and rediscover her strength.

Each of these stories highlights different paths to resilience—whether it's overcoming self-doubt, adapting to unexpected challenges, or learning to ask for support. Their experiences remind us that growth often comes from moments of struggle and that resilience is built through intentional choices and actions.

Living Resiliently

Resilience is not about avoiding life's challenges but about thriving despite them. Thriving might look like finding joy in small victories, maintaining meaningful relationships, or building routines that support both your personal and professional growth. It's about living fully and authentically, even in the face of adversity. It involves grounding ourselves in self-compassion, embracing imperfection, and taking actionable steps toward growth.

Steps to Strengthen Your Resilience

- **Adopt a Growth Mindset:** View challenges as opportunities to gain experience rather than obstacles.

- **Revisit Your Core Values:** Grounding yourself in what truly matters can help keep you focused during challenging times. For example, if one of your core values is family, remind yourself of how your resilience can positively impact your loved ones. Reflecting on these values provides motivation and clarity when obstacles arise.

- **Develop Healthy Coping Mechanisms:** Engaging in activities like journaling, meditating, or exercising can help you process emotions constructively.

Author Spotlight:
Viktor Frankl and the Power of Meaning

In *Man's Search for Meaning*, Viktor Frankl shares his profound insights on resilience and purpose, born from his experiences in concentration camps. He writes: "When we are no longer able to change a situation, we are challenged to change ourselves."

Frankl's teachings highlight the power of reframing adversity as an opportunity to find meaning and growth. His work serves as a reminder that resilience is not just about enduring challenges but transforming them into catalysts for purpose and fulfillment.

Closing Thoughts:
In Rising Through the Challenges

Setbacks reveal strength we often don't realize we possess. Each challenge holds a lesson, helping us grow, recalibrate, and thrive.

When life pulls you back, think of it as a slingshot. With each setback, you're being prepared to launch forward with greater force. The tools of resilience—self-compassion, reflection, and adaptability—transform each pullback into a launch forward, propelling you to soar higher than before. Remember the opening question—those moments when you feel pulled back? Use these tools of resilience to rise above them, turning those moments into opportunities for growth and transformation. The tools of resilience—self-compassion, reflection, and adaptability—will help you rise and continue your journey.

As you embrace resilience, you prepare yourself not only to face life's challenges but to rise above them. Ahead, we'll explore how to move beyond resilience into a state of thriving that is rooted in peace, purpose, and fulfillment.

CHAPTER NINE:

BEYOND THE BATTLE

> *The greatest victory is not in winning every battle, but in rising every time we fall.*—**Confucius**

When was the last time you paused and asked yourself: *Why am I still fighting this battle?* Whether it's a tug-of-war for perfection, validation, or approval, we often cling to struggles that no longer serve us. But what if you didn't have to hold the rope at all?

This chapter challenges you to imagine a life where peace replaces struggle, joy outweighs achievement, and fulfillment isn't something you chase—it's something you live.

Here, we'll shift focus from striving and surviving to flourishing in harmony with yourself. By letting go of the need for struggle, you allow joy, alignment, and fulfillment to guide your life.

The Shift from Fighting to Thriving

Once we've faced the battles of self-doubt, boundary-setting, and people-pleasing, it's natural to feel a sense of exhaustion. Yet, there's an even deeper freedom available to us: the ability to thrive without feeling we need to fight at all.

Thriving doesn't mean life becomes perfect or free from challenges—it means facing those challenges with a sense of inner steadiness and trust. It's the feeling of being grounded, even when life throws curveballs, because your sense of worth isn't tied to external circumstances.

Thriving is a state of embracing and celebrating life as it is. It means waking up with a sense of purpose, feeling joy in small moments, and having the energy to pursue passions and relationships. In relationships, thriving might mean fostering open communication and mutual respect, creating bonds that nurture both parties. In self-care, it could be as simple as prioritizing rest or pursuing hobbies that spark joy.

Living fully is a choice you make daily. It's choosing to let go of battles that drain you and to invest in actions and relationships that nourish you. It's saying yes to what aligns with your values and no to what pulls you away from them.

By allowing our inner peace and self-worth to guide our actions rather than a need for external approval, alignment becomes a natural way of being. At the heart of this transformation is self-compassion. It's giving yourself permission to rest, to enjoy life's simple pleasures, and to accept that you are enough—just as you are. When we treat ourselves with kindness, we naturally experience more peace and joy in our lives.

Take a moment to picture what thriving might look like for you. Imagine waking up without the weight of proving yourself to others. What would you do differently? How would your relationships change? What passions or hobbies would you pursue if there was no pressure to achieve or compete?

It's a profound difference—surviving versus truly living. When we release the compulsion to "win" or to prove ourselves, we find that life's richness comes from simple presence, joyful engagement, and inner alignment. This freedom allows us to embrace each moment as it comes, finding meaning in being, rather than achieving.

Moving Toward Harmony

Living in harmony is about balance and acceptance. It's finding ways to meet life with openness, responding to criticism with curiosity instead of defensiveness or embracing changes as opportunities rather than setbacks.

While balance often feels like a precarious act of holding everything together, harmony allows us to let go of tension and embrace a natural rhythm.

This openness frees us from the need to fight, defend, or prove. This state of harmony is a place where we feel deeply aligned with our values and connected to our purpose, yet free to flow with whatever comes our way.

Example: Maya, once a constant overachiever, learned to release her need for perfection and external validation. One day, she found herself staying late at work again to meet a deadline. She paused and asked, *"Who am I doing this for?"* That moment became her turning point. By setting boundaries and focusing on what truly mattered, she found a newfound harmony. She still pursued her passions but did so from a place of inner balance rather than striving for others' approval.

Living Beyond the Tug-of-War

Living beyond the constant push and pull means releasing the need to shape ourselves according to others' expectations. It means no longer feeling bound to please everyone or seeking validation from sources outside us. Instead, it's about coming into harmony with our own truths and living in a way that reflects our deepest values.

The real victory isn't in defeating an opponent but in realizing there's no opponent at all. The moment you release the need for external validation, the fight dissolves, leaving only you—strong, whole, and at peace.

Guiding Principles for Thriving:

- **Accept Your Unique Journey:** Embrace that your life is uniquely yours, free from the need to meet others' timelines or standards.

- **Allow Authenticity:** Permit yourself to live according to your values, no longer adapting to fit someone else's version of success.

- **Focus on Inner Fulfillment:** Measure success by your internal peace, happiness, and alignment with who you genuinely are.

Personal Reflections on Moving Beyond the Battle

1. **Reflect on Your Source of Peace:** Think about a specific habit, place, or activity that consistently brings you peace. For example, is it morning meditation, a walk in nature, or time spent with loved ones? How can you integrate more of these moments into your daily routine?

2. **Identify Areas of Harmony:** Reflect on aspects of your life where you already feel a sense of balance. What's working well, and how can you bring this harmony into other areas?

3. **Release a Source of Struggle:** Identify a remaining struggle that feels like a battle. Consider how you might gradually let it go and welcome peace in its place.

Creating a New Definition of Success and Happiness

For many of us, success has been defined by external-marker career achievements, social status, or financial security. Yet, authentic success is something deeply personal. It's about contentment, fulfillment, and living a life that feels true. When we redefine success, we begin to experience happiness as a constant presence rather than a destination.

Redefining Success and Happiness:

- **Success as Alignment:** Begin measuring success by how closely your daily life reflects your core values.

- **Happiness as Presence:** See happiness as the ability to be fully present, finding joy in simple, meaningful moments rather than future achievements.

- **Growth as a Journey, Not a Goal:** Embrace growth as an ongoing journey rather than striving for perfection or finality.

Example: Nina once equated success with corporate advancement. Over time, she realized these markers didn't bring her the happiness she'd anticipated. She redefined success as a life that allowed her to balance time with her family, pursue personal interests, and enjoy her work. Her happiness became a daily experience of contentment rather than a distant achievement.

Empowerment Actions

1. **Daily Practice of Mindfulness:** Begin each day by simply observing your thoughts, noticing any tendencies toward judgment or stress. Set an intention to carry a feeling of calm throughout the day.

2. **Set Boundaries for Peace:** Protect your inner peace by gently setting boundaries with people or activities that drain your energy.

3. **Cultivate a Gratitude Habit:** At the end of each day, reflect on a few things you're grateful for. This simple practice can help shift your focus from what's missing to what is fulfilling and abundant.

Stories of Thriving Beyond the Battle

- **Caleb's Transformation:** Caleb left a high-stress job to pursue writing, a quiet passion he'd held for years. Despite facing doubts and skepticism, Caleb found deep satisfaction and peace in this new chapter. No longer seeking external validation, he experienced true freedom simply enjoying his work each day.

- **Ivy's Release:** Ivy used to view life as a series of struggles. After realizing the toll this mindset was taking on her well-being, she shifted her focus from competition to collaboration. By embracing others' successes and setting clear boundaries, Ivy transformed her life from one of constant striving to one of connection and contentment.

Letting Go of the Battle Mindset

The decision to live without constant struggle means letting go of the belief that life must be a series of battles. By embracing harmony, we create space for peace, joy, and meaningful connection. Letting go of the battle mindset doesn't mean giving up; it means trusting that you are enough without the constant struggle. This shift can feel uncomfortable at first, as we've often tied our worth to how hard we fight. Yet, on the other side of discomfort lies freedom.

Metaphor for Transformation

Letting go of the battle mindset is like putting down a heavy backpack you've carried for years. At first, it feels strange to walk without it, but soon you realize how light and free you are, able to move forward with ease.

Practical Steps

- Identify one area of life where you feel locked in a

battle. Ask yourself: *"What am I fighting for, and is it truly serving me?"*

- Explore small ways to release control—whether it's stepping back from a toxic relationship, saying no to a draining obligation, or simply allowing yourself to rest without guilt.

The more we release the need to fight, the more space we create for harmony and joy. Flourishing isn't about winning battles, it's about choosing peace and alignment, moment by moment.

Author Spotlight:
Thich Nhat Hanh and *Peace Is Every Step*

Thich Nhat Hanh's work on mindfulness and presence offers a powerful lens for understanding what it means to live liberated. In his book, *Peace Is Every Step*, he emphasizes that true peace comes from within and is cultivated by releasing resistance and embracing the present moment. He writes, "When we are mindful, deeply in touch with the present moment, our understanding of what is going on deepens, and we begin to be filled with acceptance, joy, peace, and love."

His teachings remind us that flourishing isn't about fighting against life's challenges but about accepting them with awareness. For example, instead of reacting with frustration to an unexpected obstacle, practicing mindfulness allows us to *pause, breathe, and respond with clarity rather than resistance*. Small shifts—such as slowing down, practicing gratitude, and fully engaging in the present—can create profound changes in how we experience joy and inner alignment.

Thich Nhat Hanh's insights remind us that moving beyond the battle means embracing our authentic selves and allowing mindfulness to guide our choices, moment by moment.

What is Integrity?

Integrity, as Martha Beck describes, is living in alignment with our true values and desires rather than the expectations imposed by others. It's the antidote to the inner conflict that arises when our actions don't match our beliefs.

Practical Strategy

Beck suggests starting with small, honest actions that reflect your inner truth. For example, if you feel drained in a relationship, a step toward integrity might involve expressing your needs clearly and compassionately.

Connection to Flourishing

When we act from a place of integrity, the battle mindset fades. Instead of fighting for approval or struggling to meet external demands, we thrive by honoring who we truly are. This creates a life of alignment, joy, and peace.

Closing Thoughts:

Embracing Life Beyond the Battle

As you step into this new phase of your journey, recognize that you have the power to release the need for constant struggle. You've built resilience, learned to thrive beyond validation, and cultivated an inner peace that is yours to keep.

Embrace the life you've created, one where you can thrive without always feeling the need to fight. As you move forward, revisit the reflections in this chapter and choose one action to implement today—whether it's setting a boundary, practicing gratitude, or exploring your definition of success.

The journey to self-discovery and fulfillment is ongoing, but each step forward reflects your courage and commitment to a life of harmony.

Abraham Lincoln wisely said, *"The best way to predict your future is to create it."* Beyond the tug-of-war lies a world of infinite possibility; a life waiting to be lived fully and authentically.

As we step into the concluding chapter, we'll explore how to integrate all you've learned, embracing the journey as a whole. Together, we'll celebrate your growth, set intentions for the future, and step forward with courage and clarity.

CHAPTER TEN:

BREAK FREE, BE YOU

"

Be yourself; everyone else is already taken. **—Unknown**

"

*A*s you turn the final pages of this journey, take a moment to reflect on how far you've come. This isn't just a book, it's a companion, a guide, and a mirror reflecting your deepest truths. Together, we've unraveled the ropes of self-doubt, fear, and societal expectations that have held you back for so long. Each chapter has been a step toward reclaiming your power, unveiling insights and strategies that align your life with your true self. Together, these lessons have built a foundation for the next phase of your journey, one filled with intention and authenticity.

This chapter is about celebrating the progress you've made, envisioning the possibilities ahead, and embracing a life free from unnecessary battles. It's not about perfection but about authenticity—choosing to live fully, boldly, and unapologetically as yourself.

Your Journey of Liberation

Breaking free doesn't mean you won't face challenges. It means you've chosen courage over fear, authenticity over conformity, and self-love over external validation. The battles you've fought—against guilt, perfectionism, and people-pleasing—were the foundation of your transformation, not just obstacles in your path.

Breaking free means no longer apologizing for who you are. It's the relief of shedding the weight of expectations that were never yours to carry and the joy of finally standing tall in your truth. There may be moments of vulnerability as you step into this new way of being, but with every step, you'll feel lighter and more aligned with your values.

The real victory isn't in winning the tug-of-war; it's in letting go of the rope entirely. You've discovered that peace, joy, and authenticity are not prizes to be won but gifts to be embraced. Each step you've taken to set boundaries, practice gratitude, and redefine success has built a foundation for a life that reflects your values and aspirations.

The Power of Choice

Every decision you make from this moment forward is an opportunity to align your life with your values and joy. For instance, setting a boundary with a friend or dedicating time each day to a passion project can be small but powerful declarations of your truth. Breaking free isn't a one-time event, its practice, a daily declaration of your worth, and a commitment to honoring your truth.

Principles for Living Authentically:

- Release the Need to Prove: Your value is inherent, not something to be earned or validated by others.

- Celebrate Progress Over Perfection: Growth isn't linear or flawless, but it's yours. Honor the journey, not just the destination.

- Trust in Your Path: Your life is uniquely yours, and the steps you take—no matter how small—are leading you to greater freedom and fulfillment.

Life Worth Living

What does it mean to live fully? It's not about striving for perfection or avoiding every difficulty but about creating a life that feels deeply meaningful. Letting go of external expectations can feel daunting, but each step you take toward prioritizing your values strengthens your sense of fulfillment and peace.

Living fully might mean cherishing quiet mornings with loved ones, pursuing creative passions, or finding joy in daily routines that reflect your values. When you release the need to please and instead focus on pleasing yourself, you create space for what truly matters: love, connection, growth, and fulfillment.

You've already proven your strength by reaching this point in the journey. Every choice you make from here forward is a testament to your courage and determination to live authentically. Trust in your ability to navigate whatever comes next.

Imagine This

You wake up on a crisp morning, sunlight streaming through your window. Instead of rushing to meet others' expectations, you savor a moment of stillness. You sip coffee, journal about your intentions for the day, and prioritize activities that bring you joy and alignment. Your schedule is filled with meaningful work, quality time with loved ones, and space for rest and reflection. The tension of trying to be everything to everyone is gone, replaced by quiet confidence in your choices.

That afternoon, you're at a gathering with friends, and for the first time in years, you feel no need to impress anyone. Instead, you speak your mind openly, sharing stories and laughter without hesitation. Someone asks your opinion on a topic, and you answer confidently, without fearing judgment or needing validation. You realize in that moment how far you've come: you've shed the mask of perfection and embraced the beauty of being unapologetically yourself.

This is the life of someone who has let go of the tug-of-war.

Personal Reflections

Take a moment to reflect on these questions:

1. What are you proud of in your journey so far?

2. What practices will help you continue honoring your values and authenticity? Identify one practice you can commit to this week to honor your values and authenticity.

3. What legacy do you want to create—not just for others, but for yourself? How can your journey inspire others to follow their own path?

Your legacy isn't just what you leave behind, it's the impact your choices have on the world around you. When you live authentically, you give others permission to do the same. Your courage to break free creates a ripple effect, inspiring friends, family, and even strangers to examine their own lives and embrace their truths.

Your Charge:
Break Free, Be You

As you close this chapter, know that this is not an ending; it's a beginning. The journey of living authentically is ongoing, filled with opportunities for growth, connection, and joy. Each choice you make, no matter how small, is a declaration of your freedom and a testament to your strength.

Revisit the practices and reflections from earlier chapters to reinforce your growth and stay aligned with your authentic path, recognizing that each moment of self-awareness adds to the mosaic of your transformation. Even if setbacks occur, remember that each day is a chance to recommit to your truth.

Remember, the journey of breaking free isn't always linear. There will be days when old habits or doubts resurface, and that's okay. Each moment offers a new opportunity to choose yourself repeatedly. Progress isn't about being perfect, it's about continuing to show up for yourself.

A Week in the Life of Living Free

Monday morning begins with gratitude journaling and a brisk walk in the park. You set clear priorities for the day, balancing work tasks with time for yourself. At lunch, you meet a friend who energizes you with laughter and meaningful conversation. By evening, you've completed your work, leaving space to enjoy a favorite hobby.

Midweek, you encounter a challenge at work but respond with confidence and clarity. You express your boundaries respectfully, ensuring your workload remains manageable. Afterward, you reflect on the day, recognizing your progress in handling demanding situations.

The weekend is a mix of relaxation and connection. You visit family, savoring shared moments without the need to overextend yourself. On Sunday evening, you prepare for the week ahead with a renewed sense of purpose and alignment.

This life isn't free from challenges, but it's filled with intention, balance, and joyful reflection of your commitment to thriving.

For instance, consider starting your day with a simple five-minute meditation to center yourself or a gratitude practice to ground you in abundance. These small habits anchor you in the joy and peace of living authentically.

Closing Thoughts

Take a deep breath and celebrate how far you've come. This isn't just a milestone, it's a launchpad for the life you're building. Celebrate your journey and envision the ever-expanding possibilities that lie before you. Each step is a testament to the growth and transformation you've embraced.

It's important to celebrate not just the milestones but the quiet, unseen moments of resilience—every time you chose yourself over external expectations, every boundary you set, every time you stood firm in your truth. These moments are the threads of the authentic life you've woven.

Whenever you need a reminder of your strength, return to these pages as a source of guidance and inspiration.

A LETTER
TO THE READER

Dear Reader,

Thank you for taking this journey with me. Writing this book was not just an act of creation but one of connection—with you and with the truths we all hold within. I hope the pages you've read have offered clarity, encouragement, and the tools to step into your own power.

Remember, the journey to self-discovery and fulfillment doesn't end here. It evolves with each decision, each challenge, and each moment of courage you embrace. Trust that you have everything you need within you to live fully and freely.

May this book serve as a reminder of your resilience, a celebration of your authenticity, and a guide when you need one. The world is brighter because you're in it, shining your unique light. Step boldly into the life that's waiting for you; you are enough, and you are ready.

With gratitude and hope,

Marie

Congratulations on breaking free and stepping into your truth. Let this chapter mark the beginning of a life lived with intention, peace, and fulfillment. The world needs your voice, your truth, and your light.

APPENDIX A: RECOMMENDED READING

A thoughtfully curated selection of books to deepen your journey toward authenticity, resilience, and empowerment. Each title has been chosen for its ability to inspire, challenge, and guide readers in their personal growth. These works resonate with the themes explored in *Tug-of-War: Me vs. Them*, offering additional perspectives and tools for living a liberated life.

Recommended Reading List

Brown, Brené. *Daring Greatly: How the Courage to Be Vulnerable Transforms the Way We Live, Love, Parent, and Lead.* New York: Avery, 2012.

Brené Brown explores how vulnerability fosters connection and courage, aligning beautifully with the journey of embracing your authentic self.

Clear, James. *Atomic Habits: An Easy & Proven Way to Build Good Habits & Break Bad Ones*. New York: Avery, 2018.

This book provides actionable advice on creating small, sustainable changes that lead to big transformations, and a practical guide for overcoming internal struggles.

Frankl, Viktor E. *Man's Search for Meaning*. Boston: Beacon Press, 1946.

A timeless exploration of resilience and purpose, Frankl's reflections remind us of the power of reframing adversity into growth opportunities.

Hanh, Thich Nhat. *Peace Is Every Step: The Path of Mindfulness in Everyday Life*. New York: Bantam Books, 1991.

This gentle guide to mindfulness helps readers find peace and clarity, echoing the themes of reflection and intentional living.

Holiday, Ryan. *The Obstacle Is the Way: The Timeless Art of Turning Trials into Triumph*. New York: Portfolio, 2014.

Drawing on Stoic philosophy, this book demonstrates how to turn adversity into an advantage, reinforcing resilience and growth.

Kabat-Zinn, Jon. *Wherever You Go, There You Are: Mindfulness Meditation in Everyday Life*. New York: Hyperion, 1994.

A classic on mindfulness, this work encourages embracing the present moment as a foundation for personal growth and liberation from societal expectations.

Lewis, C.S. *The Screwtape Letters.* New York: HarperOne, 1942.

This fictional satire delves into the internal tug-of-war between human desires and values, offering profound reflections on morality and choice.

Sincero, Jen. *You Are a Badass: How to Stop Doubting Your Greatness and Start Living an Awesome Life.* Philadelphia: Running Press, 2013.

With humor and insight, Sincero encourages breaking free from limiting beliefs and pursuing life with confidence and passion.

Vanzant, Iyanla. *Acts of Faith: Daily Meditations for People of Color.* New York: Fireside, 1993.

A collection of daily affirmations and reflections that inspire courage, self-love, and spiritual growth, deeply resonating with themes of empowerment.

Williamson, Marianne. *A Return to Love: Reflections on the Principles of a Course in Miracles.* New York: HarperOne, 1992.

This book emphasizes the transformative power of love and forgiveness, providing spiritual insights into healing and self-discovery.

Further Exploration

For readers looking to expand their journey of self-discovery, consider exploring these additional avenues:

- **Workshops and Seminars:** Attend mindfulness retreats or workshops, such as those offered by the Omega Institute, for immersive learning experiences. Explore online courses by Brené Brown to deepen your understanding of vulnerability and courage.

- **Podcasts:** *The Minimalists Podcast* by Joshua Fields Millburn and Ryan Nicodemus – Insights on simplifying life and focusing on what truly matters. *On Being* with Krista Tippett – Conversations that explore meaning, connection, and personal growth. *Unlocking Us* by Brené Brown – Honest discussions about relationships, courage, and authenticity.

- **Journaling and Reflection**: Create a journal dedicated to reflecting on authenticity and resilience. Use prompts like:
- "What values are most important to me?" "What relationships bring me the most joy?"

- **Guided Meditations and Apps:** Explore meditation apps such as Calm or Insigh timer to develop practices that align with mindfulness and intentional living.

- **Online Communities:** Join groups on platforms like Meetup or Facebook centered on personal growth, boundary-setting, or mindfulness.

Stay Connected

Workshops and seminars, podcasts, and online journaling will soon be available through my website. Stay tuned for updates and join our growing community of individuals dedicated to personal growth and empowerment.

ACKNOWLEDGMENTS

*T*hey say it takes a village, and my village is large and full of love, support, and unwavering belief in me.

To my loving husband, Ronald Bridges, your steadfast love and encouragement have been my guiding light.

To my late mother, Cynthia Louise Holloman; my grandmothers, Caroline Ketchum and Effie B. Holloman; my grandfather, Carlton Ketchum; my brother, Abdul Qaadir, Gregory S. Holloman; Claudette McElevne; Barbara Harris; Alice Joy Crews, your memory inspires and guides me daily.

To my biggest supporters and mentors, whom I am so blessed to have in my life and whom I call Mom: **Geraldine Holloman, Margaret Precious Bridges, and my Laverne 'Patty Bean' Tanner, who will go to the ends of the earth for me.** Your guidance, love, and sacrifices have shaped me into who I am today. And to

Mom Susie Mapp, your unwavering support, wisdom, and nurturing spirit have been a cornerstone in my life. I am forever grateful for the love and strength each of you has poured into me.

To my dad, William Holloman, who never stopped believing in me. You taught me that I can be and do anything I want as long as I always put God first. Your faith in me is my guiding star.

To my children and grandchildren, your joy and curiosity inspire me daily. You are my legacy and my greatest pride.

To my twin sister, Michelle Holloman-Tiberino, my heartbeat, who loves me unconditionally and for whom nothing is too big or small to do for me. Your presence in my life is a constant source of strength and love, to my sister Pamela Washington, a God-send. Your strength and steady presence mean the world to me. I admire your independence and how you encourage me to be myself. I'm truly grateful for you.

To my sisters-in-law, Janice Powell-Holloman and Tonya Holloman—two extraordinary women whose strength, love, and unwavering encouragement have meant the world to me. Janice, your steady presence and warmth have been a constant source of support. Tonya, your love and kindness have never wavered, and I cherish the bond we share. Thank you both for always lifting me up and reminding me of the power of family, resilience, and unconditional support.

To my brothers, Nadir Holloman, and Hasign Graham, who remind me to laugh and find joy in every moment. Your humor and companionship mean the world to me.

To my nieces and nephews—my daily smiles and constant joy—know that you are deeply loved and forever part of every page I write.

To my Aunt Marcia, Aunt Marilyn, Aunt Pearl, Uncle Thomas, Uncle Clarence, and Kimyla Boyer, thank you for being there when I needed you the most. Your support and love have been my lifeline during challenging times.

To my cousins, Gwennie Hodges and Sharon Green, for your endless inspiration and encouraging words. Your support and faith in me have been a constant source of motivation.

To my sister-Friends for Life: Ramona, Angie, Sophia, Nisaa, Pamela, Angel, Joy, Carmen, Taherrah, Rhonda, Robin, Adrienne, Bridgette, Kangi, Baddriyyah, Paula Dr. Detra Johnson, Nicole V, and Nauda. Thank you for believing in me, pushing me, and standing by my side through thick and thin. Your friendship is a treasure.

To Geo Derice, the greatest book coach I know. I am grateful beyond words for your expertise, compassion, and dedication. Thank you for believing in me, motivating me, and providing unwavering support.

Most importantly, I want to thank God, the creator of all things, who makes no mistakes. Your grace and guidance have been my foundation and strength.

Thank you all for being in my village. I am eternally grateful to each one of you.

ABOUT
THE AUTHOR

*M*arie Holloman Bridges, recipient of the 2024 Lifetime Achievement Award presented by President Joseph R. Biden Jr., is a respected author, sought-after speaker, and successful entrepreneur. A proud veteran, Marie's military service exemplifies her lifelong commitment to resilience, leadership, and community impact. She is dedicated to empowering individuals to break free from societal expectations and live authentically. Known for her relatable and compassionate approach, Marie guides people through transformative journeys of resilience, self-discovery, and personal liberation.

Her impact shines through her mentoring programs, community initiatives, and literary work, all devoted to uplifting and inspiring others to embrace their true selves. With every endeavor, Marie empowers individuals to break free from the need to please others, helping them live purposefully and create meaningful, lasting change.

With a background in psychology and over 20 years of experience in consulting and counseling, Marie has dedicated her career to helping individuals understand and navigate the complexities of interpersonal dynamics. Her current pursuit of a Ph.D. in Industrial and Organizational Psychology reflects her unwavering dedication to gaining deeper insights into human behavior and interpersonal relationships.

www.ingramcontent.com/pod-product-compliance
Lightning Source LLC
Chambersburg PA
CBHW031516270326
41930CB00006B/416